VOLKSWAGEN

Golf
GTI

Such was the interest shown in the Golf Mk3 (seen above, with its predecessors, in GTI guise) that the UK importer took a last-minute surprise decision to show the car at the 1991 Motorfair, despite the fact that it was not due to be sold in Britain until early in 1992.

Below: Richard Ide, managing director of V.A.G. (United Kingdom) Ltd., removes the covers from the ultimate hot hatch, the VR6.

VOLKSWAGEN

Golf
GTI

• FIRST AND FINEST OF THE HOT HATCHES •

Origins • Development • Sport • Buying • Servicing

IAN WAGSTAFF

Windrow *&* Greene Automotive

Published in Great Britain by
Windrow & Greene Ltd
5 Gerrard Street
London W1V 7LJ

British Library Cataloguing in Publication Data
Wagstaff, Ian
   Volkswagen Golf GTI: first and finest of the hot hatches.
   I. Title
   629.2222

ISBN 1 87200 446 6

Design: *ghk* DESIGN, Chiswick, London

Printed in Great Britain by Ashford Colour Press

Contents

Acknowledgements

This is the point where it is traditional to express gratitude. For a change, I would like to commence by apportioning blame!

It was all Edward Rowe's fault. The enthusiastic Australian who used to be a Volkswagen PR man has since gone on to greater things — well, Audis do tend to be larger. However, it was Edward who suggested to me that I should write the following pages, so it was Edward who screwed up my normal writing schedule, and if he thinks he is going to get a commission after that he will have to think again, whatever his mother's literary agent receives!

Seriously, thanks, Edward. Who else would show off his new cellular phone by calling from somewhere in the Irish Sea to keep me up-to-date with the antics of the Volkswagen Junior Rally Team?

There are many who have given their support to this project, but it is the Volkswagen PR teams on both sides of the Atlantic to whom I must really express my gratitude. Laura Warren's band at Milton Keynes have shown great patience despite my constant pestering, so thanks to Laura, Beverley, Katrine, Tracey, Paul and Graham, as well as Edward... must not forget Edward.

Every time I went to California, Larry Brown and the VW West Coast team were there with a car (it took me three trips to progress from a Fox to a GTI!) and advice. Like the Milton Keynes staff, they must have despaired of me at times, particular when I left my cheque-book holder in the afore-mentioned Fox. My thanks to Larry's former assistant, Kay Cornwall, for sorting that one out and for teaching me which kind of Los Angeles inhabitant drives which kind of Volkswagen Cabriolet. (I am glad Edward was able to keep you supplied with Yorkie bars — yes, Edward gets in everywhere.) Thanks, Larry & Co., that 1988 model launch in Monterey was the best.

I trust that the many people I am now *not* going to mention will forgive me. Their names appear in the following pages, and I hope they will take my thanks as read. I must single out John Rettie for his hospitality and help, John Stevens, and two of my editors, Denis Rea (*Practical Motorist*) and Robin Wager (*VW Motoring*), who have assisted with a chapter each. If Robin had not given me the chance to write his news pages, this book might not have happened. While on the subject of editors, my apologies to Ian Robertson, motoring editor of the Economist Intelligence Unit. I only hope that, as a two-time GTI owner, he understood why this book seemed to be continually holding up my next weighty tome for him. (I am unsure of his reaction to my publisher having asked me for a second book...)

Photographs have been taken or supplied by the following: Robert Bosch Ltd; Gordon Bruce Associates; James Bryant; John Edwards; Euro Styling; Firestone UK; Richard Grant Accessories; GTi Engineering; Hella Ltd; Impact PR; MASS: David Pipes; John Rettie; Scotford Ltd; Volkswagen AG; Volkswagen UK; Volkswagen US; Robin Wager; Richard Wagstaff; Tim Wagstaff; Graham Whittaker; the author.

It seems a cliché to end by thanking one's family, but it is only by working on projects such as this that one realises how valuable is their support. So, my love and gratitude to Gill, for her forbearance and for even coming to a Club GTI sprint at Curborough; to Tim and Richard, who at least were able to take cameras to Curborough; and to Jake, who got left behind in the kennels when we went to Curborough.

Ian Wagstaff
Chinnor, Oxon 1991

This book is dedicated to Gill, Tim and Richard, the most important people.

1 Three Rounds of Golf: Whither the Hot Hatch?

August the 29th, 1991. Startled by the strange activities taking place around it, the thoroughbred racehorse was galloping riderless towards the great wedge of cars. Standing in its path, one gained some insight into how the Russian gunners must have felt as the Light Brigade bore down on them at Balaclava.

The animal was heading towards the nearest of the medium-sized vehicles — they were at a glance identical — a car finished in one of those dark indeterminate colours much favoured by Volkswagen at the start of the 1990s. One might say that the horse had chosen well for, distinguishing it from most of the other cars, this one wore badges bearing the legend *GTI*.

Sheering away, the horse was none-too expertly caught and the motoring press, which had gathered in the early morning at Munich race-course to be shown a significant new vehicle, was able to return to the day's business. The choices offered were legion, all the cars being examples of the latest generation of Volkswagen's second great success story, *der neue* Golf.

Because the concept itself seemed new, and perhaps because the thought of a 2.8-litre V6 engine in such a small car appeared to be the ideal antidote to a heavy evening, many of those assembled jumped first into the new VR6 variant. By late morning, however, the clamour for this model had died down; anyone wanting to drive it had only to wait for the next one to be returned. By contrast, there was a queue for the next model in the line-up, which seemed to be in strangely short supply.

Having sampled the mini-Mercedes-like opulence of the VR6, the press was eager to find out what had happened to the model which 16 years earlier had made an even greater impact. Time had proved beyond any doubt or dispute that, with the GTI, Volkswagen had succeeded in producing one of the few cars which could truly justify the tag of 'legend'. How many manufacturers, after all, have created an entirely new category and given a new set of initials to the market?

Time was when the initials 'GT' had real meaning: *Gran Turismo*, Grand Touring, upmarket sports cars designed to cruise effortlessly and in comfort over great distances; one tended to think of Ferraris. Like 'sports car', it was clear what the term meant, even if no-one could perfectly define it.

Then came the marketing men, who decided to usurp said initials, debasing them for all time by giving mundane saloons the GT title. It needs a cynical mind to take letters which had applied to the likes of the Ferrari 250GT and apply them to the Ford Cortina.

However, the addition of an 'i' has made all the difference — has created a whole new meaning. A GTi is easily definable: it is a small, performance-orientated hatchback — a 'hot hatch', in current parlance. The first, the trendsetter, and still the one

*Completed behind closed factory doors, the Mk3 was
introduced to the press at Munich Race Course. It was
a fitting locale for such a thoroughbred.*

with which they are all compared, was the Volkswagen Golf GTI.

The badge on the Golf GTI is all capitals, yet
there is no hard and fast rule as to how it should be
written. Even with the launch of the third-
generation car, the information-pack from the
Offentlichkeitsarbeit Motorpresse at Wolfsburg
referred to the 'GTI', while the accompanying
press releases from the UK importer's offices in
Milton Keynes spoke of the 'GTi'.

The Golf spawned a whole generation, a host of
cars titled 'GTi', virtually all spelt that way. But,
apart from the proof they furnish of the Golf's
almost unprecedented influence, we are not concerned here with Peugeots or Mitsubishis, Rovers
or Citroens. This book unashamedly celebrates the
'GTI'.

Volkswagen was not breaking new ground by
denoting fuel injection with such a letter. Maserati
announced the very first fitting of Lucas fuel-
injection (VW uses Bosch) to a road car with the
3500GTI version of its sporting coupé. What

Volkswagen achieved was the creation of the aura
that was to surround the concept.

Basically, the company took an excellent little
family hatchback and, by giving it a performance
package, ensured that the modern successors to the
Spridget-and-Spitfire brigade were quite happy to
drive around with rear seats and other practical
considerations which their predecessors would
have spurned.

Today we have no problem in categorising the
Golf GTI, in putting it among like competitors. But
at its launch, there was nothing else like it. *Motor*
magazine listed its 'rivals' as the Ford Escort
RS2000, the Triumph Dolomite Sprint, the Renault
17TS, the Colt Galant GTO and the Alfetta 1.8 —
hardly cars with which we would now associate the
GTI.

A further abbreviation can be said to have given
birth to the GTI. 'EA337' was the code number of
the prototype Golf, and it was on this concept that
Volkswagen engineers began working in the spring
of 1973 to produce an exciting version of a simple

The Mk3 proved itself a civilised car to drive when it was launched towards the end of 1991. For all its new features, it was still visibly 'in the tradition'.

As with the other Mk3 Golfs, the GTI front seats feature a parallel-height-adjustment as standard. This means that the entire squab front and rear is moved up and down.

The GTI has been described as Herbert Schuster's 'baby'. Here Volkswagen's chief engineer, passenger car development and test, relaxes during the Mk3 launch.

family car. As will be seen in the next chapter, this was from the start an engineer's car, not a marketing man's brain-wave.

By its third manifestation, the Golf had become refined almost to the point where its origins — those pioneering test engineers were motivated by their love of motorsport — were hard to recall. Far from being unique, it was now wooing its potential buyers in a highly competitive market. Volkswagen's response to the competition has been to create a car with congenial ride, positive steering and the removal of torque steer.

The IAA '91, the Frankfurt Motor Show, witnessed a number of significant public launches, but none more so than the new Golf. The car — the environment and safety have been its midwives — looks better in the flesh than in photographs.

Pictures tend to give it a 'bread-van' look, yet the sturdy 'C' pillar does not detract from over-the-shoulder visibility. Chief designer Herbert Schäfer and his team have created a logical progression from its predecessors, with an indication that it is from a family which also includes the Polo, Passat and Corrado. The Cd figure has been reduced to 0.30.

Volkswagen's marketing supremo, Philippe Defechereux, says, 'I think the looks are more towards understatement than towards an aggressive-looking car. From the beginning, the Golf GTI has been a classless car, that can be driven by anyone from young people who are interested in "sporty" driving to the director of a bank.'

The GTI model features the new 'Plus' running-gear with optimised axle kinematics. Its six-inch alloy wheels are an understatement which bears resemblance even to some of the Mk1s. However, they are now shod with 195/50 R15 tyres. Gas-filled shock-absorbers, with matched spring/damper rates, are fitted at the rear, and the car is lowered 10mm at the front, 20mm at the back. 15-inch brake systems with discs are installed all round, internally ventilated at the front. ABS, anti-lock braking, which is standard on the VR6, is offered as an optional extra; so is the traction control system, TCS, which uses the electronic components of the anti-lock braking system. Should one side of the road be more slippery than the other, tempting one front wheel to spin, it will be braked by the TCS, which will transfer the excess drive to the other wheel.

The 'Plus' high-performance running-gear is something the GTI shares with the VR6. The front axle has been revised to eliminate troublesome drive influence on the now stiffer power-assisted steering. The 'road feedback lever arm' on which the drive forces act has been shortened considerably, from 52mm to 40mm. In addition, castor and castor offset have been increased to improve straight-ahead running and reduce sensitivity to road steering.

The new car is visibly a GTI, thanks to its black sills and wheel arch flares and its twin headlights, now under a common lens.

Europe, at last, now has a two-litre engine for the GTI. Two-litre Golfs had already been seen in the

*Above: While the GTI had grown to a full two litres
with the advent of the Mk3, the Golf range featured an
even larger engine with the six-cylinder 2.8-litre VR6
(below).*

USA and in South Africa, both countries having their own 'local' versions — Mexican, in America's case — of the performance model. (The American version was no quicker than its 1.8-litre counter- part, due to US emission regulations.)

The South Africans never had a 1.6-litre GTI (badged 'GTi' in that country), the first model of this name being built there in 1983. By the end of the 1980s, however, they were being envied their use of the unfettered 150bhp 1984cc 16-valve Passat engine for their Golf GTi 16V, sold along-side an eight-valve 1.8-litre.

A major talking-point at the introduction of the new GTI was the fact that, two-litre though it is, it would initially be available only in eight-valve form. For the time being, the 16-valve version of the Mk2 would continue in production in Yugoslavia, Mexico and South Africa.

Speaking at the launch, Professor Dr. Ing. Ulrich Seiffert, Volkswagen AG board member with responsibility for all research and development, commented: 'We can talk about production dates only when we have released the pre-production engine, which is not the case with the 16-valve. It will not be released for production until the first quarter of next year.'

Herbert Schuster, Volkswagen's chief engineer, passenger car development and test, added the next day that 'from the very beginning we had always planned to launch the 16-valve after the launch of the eight-valve, as it is to be an entirely new engine. The final output of the two-litre 16V is not yet certain. It will be somewhere in the range of 142 to 150bhp. It will be launched at the end of 1992.

'What will probably happen is that the eight-valve will increase its sales and, perhaps, a lot of people will go over to an entirely new class of vehicle, the VR6. So, when it does appear, the 16-valve will not have the importance that it might have had.'

Outside Volkswagen, it had been suggested that the 1984cc 16-valve engine had been postponed due to a lack of power and refinement.

The eight-valve GTI Mk3 derives its increased capacity from an increase of stroke from 86.4mm to 92.8mm and an increase in bore from 81.0mm to 82.5mm. Increased pulling power comes from a higher torque at a lower engine speed. As low as

The Golf VR6 brought class to the hot hatch sector. With its introduction, the GTI was no longer the ultimate mass production Golf.

The letters 'GTI', though not original, were certainly given their present meaning by Volkswagen. The decision to use a big six-cylinder engine instead of a multi-valve unit for the top-of-the-range Mk3 gave rise to a new set of initials, the VR6.

3200rpm the torque is 160Nm. The compression ratio is 10:1.

The Digifant electronic ignition and injection systems determine and correct the ignition timing for each cylinder separately. The fuel quantity is also injected in such a way that each cylinder has exactly the right amount of fuel at the right time. The integrated knock control ensures, for each individual cylinder, that the engine operates constantly just below the knock limit.

Engine and aerodynamic improvements result in a top speed of 123mph, but a 0-62mph time which, by the manufacturer's own figures, has been reduced only slightly from 10.3 to 10.1 seconds.

Though not a GTI, the new car's up-market brother, the VR6, demands one's attention. In the words of Philippe Defechereux: 'I believe that we have reached the sales ceiling for GTIs in numerical terms. The VR6 tends towards a similar direction, but what is more emphasised is that it is a more comfortable, deluxe kind of car, with a high capacity engine, low level of interior noise, very flexible gearbox, good acceleration in the higher gears, and an engine which does not have to be shifted very often.'

Herbert Schuster adds: 'I would not hesitate to call the VR6 a further progression of the GTI idea. The VR6 is a unique development. It is something which our competitors will not be able to copy for many years — like the original GTI.'

His words are echoed by those of Professor Seiffert: 'When we introduced the first GTI, we thought we had created a new vehicle class. We hope you will feel same about the VR6.'

Its level of equipment, allied to its ride, handling and 140mph, 7.6 second 0-62mph performance invite comparison with larger equipment from Stuttgart.

The heart of the car is a long-stroke six-cylinder engine with a cylinder bank angle of a mere 15 degrees. Consequently, it is able to combine the advantages of an in-line six-cylinder with those of a 60 or 90 degree design. It is short enough to be used in the customary Volkswagen transverse configuration, while allowing for the deformation zone dimensions required in case of a head-on collision, and so narrow that only one head is used. The engine was first seen in the VW Passat and was also scheduled for a mildly face-lifted Corrado.

By late 1991, General Motors and Ford had upped the hot hatch stakes with the new Astra GSi 16V (135mph) and the Escort RS2000 (129mph). By initially offering only an eight-valve model, Volkswagen had come in below its rivals with the GTI. Yet it had surely stayed ahead of the game. While everybody else was going for 16-valve

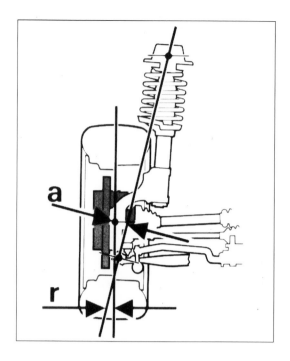

A feature of both the GTI Mk3 and VR6 is the 'Plus' running gear. This effectively suppresses the driving forces in the steering by shortening the interference force lever. Dimension 'a' is reduced from 52mm to 40mm.

heads, it had decided on two more cylinders and a much larger capacity for its top-of-the-range Golf. And by eschewing 16-valves, even if only for a time, it had focussed attention on the VR6.

The appellation 'hot hatch' seems too common to be applied to such a vehicle. And perhaps that is just as well, since even that terminology has come under fire from the Far East.

Although it was very obviously a 2+2 coupé and not a four-seater, it was claimed by Mazda at the launch of its MX-3 (also in August 1991) that it had introduced the replacement for the hot hatch. While the Japanese manufacturer was being rather wild in its claim, it was significant that it referred to the two top cars in the field as the Peugeot 205GTi and the Golf GTI. 16 years after its intro-duction, the Volkswagen was still seen by other manufacturers as a leader in its class.

In some ways, though, the entire concept of the hot hatch has changed. In its ultimate mass-production form, the hatchback is now personified by the Golf VR6: a sophisticated, comfortable grand tourer, whose size belies its class. The GTI Mk3 is itself a civilised car: get into a Mk1 and the horns grow; not so with the latest model. This is not

a criticism, however. Expectations have changed since the mid-1970s, and the GTI has changed in order to meet them.

What the GTI driver actually wants can appear confusing. In 1991, Volkswagen's own market research revealed that the most popular second choice for GTI buyers was a new BMW 3-series — which, whatever its qualities, is hardly a 'hot hatch'.

Volkswagen has not forgotten, though, the desire for raw driving pleasure which those early GTIs fulfilled. The company's answer is perhaps not a Golf, but a Polo.

By marrying its mechanically-driven 'G-lader' supercharger to the car's 1.3-litre engine, VW created what must be the spiritual successor to the first GTIs. Torque was increased by up to 50 percent, while the 113bhp (which at the car's launch in the summer of 1991 was slightly more than the then-current 1.8-litre eight-valve GTI) represented a power-to-weight ratio of 138bhp per ton. Fun to drive, nervous — and sometimes, like the Munich racehorse, with a mind of its own — the Polo G40 proves that the spirit of the original Golf GTI lives on.

The Mk3 GTI has more rounded lines and a lower Cd figure than its predecessors. The result of numerous design drafts, it looks better in the flesh than it does in photographs.

Golf GTI Mk1. '…we produced the car, presented it to the press and launched it on the market. Its success was immense.'

2 The First Generation: A New Concept

'The Golf GTI was Herr Schuster's baby,' observes Volkswagen's UK PR manager, Paul Buckett. Affable, pipe-smoking Herbert Schuster joined VW from Audi in 1975. He recalls that 'the GTI was my first car when I came to Volkswagen.

'Some preliminary work had already been carried out. These were tests done by engineers who were very interested in motor racing. They had refitted a Golf (still in its prototype stage and known as the EA337) with more powerful engines. Because of these people's racing interests, it was a very loud, very hard car.'

It already had a name, the 'Sport Golf', although 'official development had not yet started. People were just testing things out, but not within the framework of the official programme. The management was not even aware of the project.'

Schuster uses the word 'secret', but then changes it to 'unofficial'. Whatever, the work was carried out outside conventional hours.

The basis on which the engineers had to work was ideal. The Giugiaro-styled EA337 ('EA' translates into 'Development Order') materialised into the first of three generations of Volkswagen Golf. All three have used front transverse engine, front-wheel drive, independent suspension, rear torsion beam trailing arm axle, and featured a 'hatchback' body.

Volkswagen's great water-cooled success was to achieve sales of 12.7 million by the time the third generation was introduced in late 1991. It saved a company which had become too dependent on the Beetle — a design which, how ever legendary and well-loved, dated back to a commission given Professor Ferdinand Porsche as long ago as June 1934.

The Golf also had a chassis worthy of tuning, even if its potential was at first only visible to the test engineers. The body was stiff and light, the modern engine ripe for more horsepower.

Up front, MacPherson struts had been adopted, along with negative-offset steering geometry. The rear suspension was as first seen in the Volkswagen Scirocco. By locating the anti-roll bar more solidly to the trailing arms, VW had ensured that it would eliminate many of the stresses acting transversely on each arm.

Tentative approval from above first came in 1974, shortly after the standard Golf had been launched. The Sport Golf was taken to Professor Ernst Fiala, at the time Volkswagen board member responsible for development. 'He then gave the green light for the project to go ahead,' remembers Schuster, relief still in his voice after 17 years.

'Then we thought about what a production vehicle of this type might look like. What we wanted, we realised, was a car that was powerful, that drove well, but that was equally suited to everyday use. We wanted to give it good driving characteristics, but not to make it as hard as a racing car.

'We revised the style of the standard Golf and gave it its own looks. We did not want to make it

*Above: One of the original GTI publicity photographs.
This car was actually a prototype. Note the badge and
the smaller spoiler.*

*Below: 1979 saw the introduction, at last, of the
right-hand-drive GTI. The car was to remain virtually
the same for a couple of years.*

look aggressive — the main intention was for it to be more of an *understatement*' (the word is the same in German). A larger front spoiler was added, a tail spoiler being deemed unnecessary. The result was reported to reduce front end lift by 65lb at 100mph.

Initially the team had used a Solex dual-choke carburettored Audi 80GT engine. The resulting 100bhp was felt to be insufficient, but a solution was at hand.

'This was the time in the Volkswagen Group when the Bosch K-Jetronic (mechanical, driveless, continuous fuel injection) system had just been introduced,' Schuster recalls. 'Previously in the Group we had only carburettor engines.

'Even at that time, it was possible to have more torque and more power output with an injection engine.'

The belt-driven, single overhead camshaft, four-cylinder Type 827 engine from the Audi 80 was fuel injected to meet Californian exhaust emission regulations, and it was this that found its way into the Sport Golf and into the Audi 80GTE. It presented the team with a further 10bhp. Not much time had passed since 100bhp had been regarded as the power limit for front-wheel drive.

The Audi engine, with its cast-iron block and iron alloy head, had originally been 1471cc but had been stretched for the 80GT by lengthening the stroke 3mm to 79.5mm. The result was 1588cc. For the Golf GTI, new inlet and exhaust manifolds gave improved gas flow, larger-diameter valves and Heron combustion chambers recessed in piston crowns having already been used on the 80GT engine to improve breathing. The free-revving unit peaked at 6100rpm with an ignition cut-out at 7000rpm.

The smooth 110bhp engine (a 57 percent increase on the standard Golf) in a 15½cwt car 'must,' wrote the late John Bolster, 'result in a performance that, to say the least, is interesting'.

Other modifications included ventilated front disc brakes — rear discs were rejected — uprated springs and Bilstein dampers, a small, extra rear

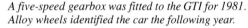

A five-speed gearbox was fitted to the GTI for 1981. Alloy wheels identified the car the following year.

*Further refinements came the way of the 1983 GTI
with a new 1.8-litre engine, higher final drive ratio
and an on-board multi-function computer.*

anti-roll bar and larger-diameter front anti-roll bar.
Wider (5 1/2-inch) wheels were fitted with 175/70
HR13 tyres replacing the standard 155-section
rubber. It was claimed that roll resistance had been
increased by 30 percent and cornering power by 12
percent. Initially, the four-speed gearbox was retained. Bolster, while feeling that the need for an
extra gear was 'not strongly felt', observed that it
might be a different matter were he to drive
regularly on the German *autobahns*.

Herbert Schuster vividly recalls one particular
hurdle, which in retrospect is hard to believe:

'It was a major difficulty within the company to
convince the people in sales that this car could be
a commercial success! A great deal of persuasion
was used, but even then they were not convinced
that the costs would not be too high.'

Thus, equipment level in the first Golf GTIs was
kept relatively low. The cheapest components from
other Golfs were used; the instrument panel, for
example, had a glove-compartment without a
cover.

In May 1975, when the Chairman of the Volkswagen Board was Toni Schmücker, the decision
was made by the Product Strategy Committee for
the Sport Golf to become an official Volkswagen
project. Even at that stage, however, its prospects
were viewed with far from unanimous optimism.

Herbert Schuster smiles. 'An interesting point to
remember is that the estimates of overall
production — not per year, but total — amounted
to just 5,000. Total!' (It should be pointed out that
5,000 was also the number needed to homologate
the GTI for Group 1 saloon car racing.)

'Then we produced the car, presented it to the
press and launched it on the market. Its success was
immense.'

No longer was there any question of the cheapest
parts being used. And as for that projected total of
5,000, there came a point where that was merely a
monthly production figure. Over one million have
now been sold.

'The cost estimation for the GTI had changed
entirely because of higher volumes. We were able

Above: Proof of the lasting appeal of the Mk1. Danny Bellamy's example had covered around 150,000 miles before it won the Slick 50 Budget Saloon Racing Championship. Here, BR Motorsport's Mick Munday samples its handling.

Below: Another example of longevity in a Mk1 GTI. Kevin Nuttall peers under the bonnet of his colourful home-tuned model.

Perhaps the most obvious hot hatch rivals to the GTI during the 1980s were the Ford Escort XR3 and XR3i. This is a 1983 example of the latter.

to put more into the car than had previously been planned.'

The developers, like Herbert Schuster, had been convinced from the very beginning that they would be able to sell far more GTIs than the sales people had predicted: 'It was such a fun car to drive. It was unequalled by any other'.

For all their misplaced pessimism, one has to feel a certain sympathy with the sales people. As Schuster concedes, 'It was an entirely new development. They had no model for their predictions.

'It was a long time before other manufacturers were able to recognise and make cars to compete with the GTI. So for a number of years, the GTI had the field to itself.'

The now-familiar name was selected by the sales department, which wanted the car to appear independent from other Golfs. 'Audi already had a GTE, so we called the Golf the GTI to differentiate between the two.'

The truly international flavour of the car was reflected in its nomenclature, 'i' standing for injection in English or *iniezione* in Italian. The 'e' remains German — *Einspritzung*. Confusingly to Anglo-Saxon ears, a German will pronounce 'i' as 'ee'!

'I remember the press presentation at the Frankfurt Show,' says Schuster. 'Most of the journalists there were very enthusiastic about the car, although there were a few critical voices. Some of them asked whether it was not irresponsible to make a small lightweight car so powerful. There were predictions that the accident rate for the GTI would be high, but fortunately, as time was to prove, this was not the case. The car has excellent safety characteristics.'

It was probably just 'talk' when one heard so-called enthusiasts stating that the continent had become littered with Golf GTIs, wheels uppermost. Nevertheless, the GTI had brought a new level of performance to a new level of customers, and they had to learn how to handle it. Other drivers who saw the all-black grille with the thin red border in their mirrors began to learn to give way.

The car on the Frankfurt stand in September 1975 was still a prototype, production versions becoming available the following June.

The press was delighted by the performance of the car, by the low-speed torque and by the fact that, despite its front-wheel drive, its handling response was largely neutral. The GTI scored over other sporting saloons in that it was actually comfortable to drive and, for the time, economical on fuel. Nor was it lost on journalists that they were witnessing the arrival of a genuinely new concept.

The car was not shown in Britain until late 1976, its first UK public appearance being at the London Motor Show. 'For technical reasons it will not be possible to produce right-hand-drive versions,' stated the importer's press release. *Motor* still described it as a 'homologation special', but added that, at £3,372, it was 'exceptional value for money... unusually cheap for a German car.' The magazine gave a 0-60mph time of 9.6 seconds and reckoned on a top speed of 108mph. These were below the manufacturer's figures of just under nine seconds and 113mph. *Motor* conceded, however, that 'VW's claims in the past have been realistic, so perhaps our test car was below par.' Fuel consumption was quoted as 28.5mpg overall.

Jeremy Walton, writing in *Motor Sport*, also had use of 'MKT 512R' from the importer's press fleet. He had been told that the car had already 'disgraced itself' with its performance figures. His comment to that was that 'it is still faster than any mass-production 1600 that I can recall.' He described it as having the kind of performance found in the 3-litre BMW saloons, with 'the agility of a 110 horsepower flea'.

Volkswagen launched early versions of the GTI to the British press by using the twisting 1127-yard Prescott hillclimb, near Cheltenham. The competition to be quickest up the hill became quite heated over the years, with Walton, no mean racing driver in his own right, the eventual champion.

The lack of competition for the first GTI was obvious. In November 1979, *What Car?* lined up the GTI against the Ford Escort RS2000, Talbot Sunbeam Ti and Vauxhall Chevette HS. 'It became obvious early on in this test that for everyday use there was only one winner — and that was a winner by some margin. The Golf GTI is truly a remarkable car...'

There had been some significant changes that year. A right-hand-drive version was made available at last and in August the GTI was fitted

The latest, German-inspired GTI rage in 1991 was dayglo 'splats'. They were said to fade fairly quickly — probably a good job too!

The Karmann-built GTI Convertible was based on the Mk1. It remained so even after introduction of the Mk2 Golf.

By 1991 Mk1 bodyshells were a rarity.
Brian Ricketts laid his hands on this example.

with a five-speed gearbox. Alloy wheels became standard for the 1980 model year, while the Golf's sister coupé, the Scirocco, dropped its GLi badge in Britain for the 1981 model year and itself became a GTI.

The top was lifted off the Golf in 1979 by Karmann, the Osnabruck company responsible for the Beetle Cabriolet. A GTI version shared the 110bhp engine of its hatchback namesake but, being 12 percent heavier, could not match its performance. Less rigid and with most of the extra weight at the rear, it could never be thought of as a true GTI. When the second generation Golf appeared in 1983, the convertibles continued to be based on the older model, or A1 as it is known in Wolfsburg. (The A class is the internal designation for the Golf, the Passat being the B class and the Polo the A Zero. This meant that, logically, the second generation was to be the A2.)

By the early 1980s the 'hot hatch' concept was established, as other manufacturers recognised that the shape could accommodate something more than just a mundane family car. In April 1981 *Autocar* named the Alfasud 1.5Ti, the Ford Escort XR3, the Renault 5 Gordini (or Alpine outside the UK) and the Sunbeam 1.6Ti, as the Golf GTI's main competitors.

The magazine even went so far as to say that 'the contest… is really between the Ford and the Volkswagen. Choosing between them depends finally on personal taste. If you are used to modern air-blending heaters, good ventilation, and prefer its still distinctive and aerodynamic looks, then it has to be the XR3, but only by a hairsbreadth. If an unusual combination of almost equally good handling and ride — the Golf rides very much better than the Escort, even if that isn't saying much — plus the most pleasing engine characteristics of the class matter more, then it is the Volkswagen, which is still a marvellous car of its size and type to drive.'

History was to prove which car would stand the test of time. The Escort XR3, improved in its better-handling injected XR3i form but less stable when it came to the last of the CVH-engined versions, the Mk5, was to lose out to the GTI in the charisma stakes. (At the Earls Court Motorfair in 1991, a month or so after the launch of the Volkswagen Golf Mk3, Ford showed it was still competing in the 'hot hatch' market: a completely new 1.8-litre XR3i made its debut, the first production car to be powered by Ford's 16-valve double overhead camshaft Zeta engine.)

Even in 1981, former Le Mans winner Paul Frere wrote in *Road & Track* that the XR3 could not equal the performance of the GTI. He reckoned, though, that serious competition was emerging in the shape of the Fiat Ritmo (Strada in the UK) Abarth and the turbocharged Renault 5 Alpine. Volkswagen of France was sufficiently worried by the challenge to market the GTI 16S, a 136bhp, twin-cam, 16-valve crossflow conversion from the German tuning concern, Oettinger.

A factory increase in horsepower came in August 1982, and with fuel-injected XR3i and Vauxhall Astra/Opel Kadett models scheduled, it was timely. The bore was increased to 81mm and the stroke to 86.4mm. The result was 1781cc and

112bhp. A new crankshaft of longer throw had to be fitted, while balancing was improved and a torsional vibration damper introduced. The combustion chamber shape was also slightly altered, thanks to VW's research into lean-burn technology. The compression ratio was altered to 10:1.

If the power had increased only a little, the boosted torque had provided greater flexibility and mid-range acceleration. 'This,' said Michael Scarlett in *Autocar*, 'is one of those rare engines that never seem short of urge.' Top speed rose only to 114mph, but a 0-60mph time of 8.2 seconds could now be claimed. The price in the UK was now £6,499.

'At the risk of sounding interminably repetitious,' said *Motor*, 'the GTI still rules.' However, a new model was now only a year away. It was heralded by the last of the Mk1 GTIs, the now sought-after Campaign model with its four-headlamp grille, sliding steel sunroof and 6Jx14 alloy wheels with 185/60HR14 Pirelli P6 tyres. Demand for the first generation had always outstripped supply in Britain, but by the end of its life UK sales amounted to 16,890.

Pressing on with a Mk1. Some late models featured twin headlamp grilles.

Wolfsburg in Germany — famed home of the Golf.
The plant is said to be the size of 350 football pitches.

*Golf GTI Mk2 16V. An impressive increase in power
helped to keep the GTI at the top of the hot hatch
league. This is a 1989 example.*

3 The Second Generation: Retaining the Basic Concept

'The GTI now has many competitors, some called "GTi" because we never patented the name as a trade-mark,' reflects Herbert Schuster. 'It would have been better if we had.'

Certainly, by the time the 'A2' or 'second generation' Golf was shown to the press in Munich during August 1983, the GTI was no longer a unique vehicle but one of a whole group of GTEs, XRs and — some manufacturers have no imagination — GTis.

Volkswagen's response was to introduce a GTI version of the new Golf — which had been developed at a cost of some £250 million — right at the beginning of 1984.

Schuster: 'The idea was to retain the basic concept of the first generation GTI, a car that should be fun to drive, a powerful car with good handling and driving characteristics, but on the other hand, also a comfortable car with low interior noise, and good for everyday use.'

The less angular body of the new car had a drag co-efficient of 0:34, as against the previous car's 0:40. With a kerb weight of 2063lb, it was some 210lb heavier than the Mk1, being 6.7 inches longer, 2.2 inches wider, and with a wheelbase extended by 3 inches. The old car had been criticised by some for its cramped accommodation; now Volkswagen had the opportunity of widening the market for the GTI by attracting those for whom use of the rear seats was essential.

Work on the 1.8-litre engine had resulted in an improved peak torque figure of 114lb/ft at 3100 rpm; peak power, while remaining at 112bhp, was now achieved at 5500rpm instead of 5800rpm. Acceleration was very slightly down, though still with a 0-60mph time of below nine seconds, and VW was claiming a maximum speed of 119mph. Fuel consumption was now over 30mpg.

Nor had comments on the Mk1's brakes gone unheeded. Discs were now fitted all round, while the right-hand-drive cars had the brake servo-master cylinder operated directly by pedal, rather than by a lengthy cross-linkage. A larger 8.3in diameter clutch was installed. Grip, too, was improved with 185/60HR14 Pirelli P6 tyres, as had been found on the Mk1 Campaign model. The GTI could now put as much low profile rubber on the road as its competitors.

The excellent suspension of the original car was little changed, the wheel travel being increased for a better ride and less road noise. The handling was pleasingly neutral at modest speeds and easy to control when going faster.

The Mk2 came in at £7,687 in Britain, which put it at something of a disadvantage. The Astra GTE was £6,995 and the Escort XR3i only £6,777. *Motor* compared the trio with the GTI Mk1. 0-60mph times were recorded of 8.3 seconds for the new car, 8.1 for the old, 8.5 for the Vauxhall, and 8.6 for the Ford. At that speed there was little in it, but the chase for 100mph told a different story. The new GTI won hands down, its time of 26.6

*Above: Golf GTI Mk2.
The new car retained its
predecessor's fine ride
and handling. Steering,
though, was heavier and
more prone to
torque-steer effects.*

*Left: As with the Mk1,
Bosch K-Jetronic fuel
injection was at the
heart of the Mk2 GTI.
However, the metering
unit was now mounted
on the other side of the
engine bay.*

Above: Under the bonnet of an early Mk2. The power was still 112bhp, though at 5,500rpm as against the 5,800rpm of the Mk1.

Right: What else could this be with a gear-knob like that? The driver's functional working-space in a Mk2.

seconds comparing with 28.8 (Mk1), 30.3 (Astra) and 28.3 (XR3i). The Mk2's fourth and fifth gear acceleration was also vastly better than its rivals.

January 1985 brought a product uprating for the GTI, with twin headlights, two-into-one exhaust pipes and new interior trim. The UK was at last offered a five-door model, its specification being the same as the three-door version.

The next step was significant in the annals of the car as, for the first time, two mainstream versions were made available.

A factory 16-valve engine for the Golf and Scirocco had first been seen in public at the 1983 Frankfurt Show, although it should be remembered that both Oettinger and Austrian tuners Graf had already produced 16-valve heads.

In a story that was to be echoed by the launch of the third generation car, Volkswagen's own 16-valve engine did not immediately become available. Doubtless this was a relief to its competitors, who would have seen a freer revving, better-breathing GTI as a serious threat.

Officially, production delays were attributed to the need to meet increasingly stringent emission controls. Unofficially, it was whispered that the 16-valve engine was initially too noisy and un-refined. Cracked heads, also, were all-too common. Whatever, by late 1985 the engine had been sorted, though British enthusiasts had to wait until early the following year to buy the new Golf GTI 16V. The era of the multi-valve engine, the answer to forced induction, had begun.

The still-1781cc engine featured an entirely new light alloy four valves-per cylinder head. The valves were operated by hydraulic tappets for re-duced maintenance, while the twin camshafts were driven by a linked steel chain. Originally a gear drive between the camshafts had been used, but the chain proved a quieter solution. The engine bay was dominated by a large fuel injection plenum chamber sited neatly atop the new cylinder head.

For a twin overhead camshaft unit, the head had an unusual valve layout. The 33mm sodium-filled exhaust valves were vertical, while the paired 40mm inlet valves were inclined at 25 degrees from the vertical. This enabled the head to be kept relatively narrow and allowed for an efficient mixture burn. Self-adjusting hydraulic tappets

The Mk2 featured twin headlights, but Motor *magazine asked why there were no headlamp washers.*

Club GTI member Paul Renshaw tests the agility of his Mk2.

were also used, giving consistent valve clearance.

The result was an impressive increase in power over the 8-valve GTI to 139bhp (or 129bhp where a catalytic converter was fitted) and an improvement in torque to 124lb/ft at 4600rpm. The close ratio gearbox of the conventional GTI was retained, with the fifth gear slightly lowered. The car was also lowered by 10mm, having revised spring and damper rates, as well as a thicker anti-roll bar. Larger pistons were used for the four-wheel disc brakes.

Autocar laid its hands on a personal import, prior to the UK launch, and found that it reached 60mph from a standing start in exactly eight seconds. With the lowered, more performance-orientated fifth gear, top speed was found to be 123mph. Particularly impressive was the 'staggering' reduction in the 70-90mph time — now just 8.4 seconds.

Once again, the GTI was able to score over its rivals. Writing in *Motor*, Roger Bell took it head-to-head with the Ford Escort RS Turbo. The GTI 16V came out as being more practical, 'relatively easy to drive and forgiving to the inexperienced'. A decade on from its inception, and the GTI was still leading its class.

The 16-valve was slow in coming to Britain. In October 1985, the importer wrote to the sales managers of its franchise dealers stating that 'the ever-elusive Golf GTI 16-valve is proving even more elusive. We are disappointed to tell you that production of the right-hand-drive version will not commence before April next year. Left-hand-drive models will also be affected by the delay.'

Late in 1986 it was stated that production of the 16-valve engines for the Golf and Scirocco was to be increased from 250 to 400 units a day. Fifty percent of GTI orders were now for the £10,636 16-valve model.

Other changes saw the adoption of optional power-assisted steering in 1986 and the introduction of ABS — anti-lock braking — again as an optional extra, on left-hand-drive models. By the following February, both the GTI and GTI 16V were benefiting from this safety improvement.

The total number of Golfs of all kinds exceeded the nine million mark in 1987, the landmark car being an eight-valve GTI fitted with a catalyser. By then, GTIs had become the most popular version of the Golf in the UK, accounting for 29 percent of total sales. In the first six months of 1987, sales were up 67 percent on the previous year and included 1,600 of the new 16-valve. A year later, sales of UK GTIs were again up 35 percent to 11,562.

Above and below: The advent of a multi-valve GTI called for separate badging for the two models.

Volkswagen introduced special equipment packages for both the eight- and 16-valve GTIs in 1988, the idea being to celebrate the production of the 10 millionth Golf. Included were seven-spoke alloy wheels, half-darkened rear light clusters and three metallic paint colours. Inside, multi-striped upholstery, central locking and uprated Blaupunkt stereos were to be found.

MG Maestro poster advertising that year announced that 'The Golf will be along in a second'. Perhaps it should have added that it was worth waiting for.

The eight-valve versions had been available in three- and five-door variants for some time, and there was felt to be an equally strong demand for this choice from 16-valve owners. The 1990 model range consequently featured a five-door variant, as well as partially colour-keyed bumper assemblies with new spoilers front and rear, the former with fog-lamps included.

The next development of the GTI was to disappoint the British, for it was decided to produce it only in left-hand-drive form. This had also been the case with the original GTI, of course, but then the importer had brought pressure to bear for the decision to be reversed. The same was not to happen with the Golf GTI G60.

The first fitting of Volkswagen's G-lader to a Golf had been in the Rallye Golf, a 5,000-only,

Right: The 16-valve head for the GTI was entirely new. Beneath the head was the familiar 1.8-litre engine GTI owners had come to admire. Peak power was up from 112 to 139bhp.

Below: The Mk2 GTI 16V was a flier. Even with a catalyst exhaust system, it still had 129bhp on tap.

four-wheel-drive homologation special. Use had been made of VW's syncro-system and its own supercharger in a vain attempt to achieve World Championship Rally success.

The G-lader, or G-shaped supercharger, is an old idea revived, which uses the eccentric rotation of a displacer within a double spiral to compress the air. Volkswagen engineers greatly prefer it to the now common turbocharger. It is less complicated in construction, has fewer parts and less heat build-up. It also provokes instant response. Using it, VW reckons to produce 2.6-litre performance from a 1.8-litre engine.

The G-lader joined the GTI for early 1990, the result being a 160bhp, 135mph 'ultimate' GTI. Torque was increased 34 percent to 166lb/ft at 3800rpm, and all this was achieved using the eight-valve engine.

The character of the car was much changed from the GTI 16V. There was less need for gear-changing or for keeping the revs high. The 20mm front and 10mm rear reduction in ride height did not detract from the car's ride quality. Standard rubber was 185/55 R15V with an 'Edition' package on offer which included BBS 6.5in wheels with 195/50 R15V tyres.

As an aside, it is worth noting that by mid-1991 the GTI 16V was considered sufficiently high performance by Pirelli to warrant a 205/50 ZR15 application of its asymmetric P Zero tyre. The motorsport-developed P Zero had first been used as original equipment for the 201mph Ferrari F40.

As stated, the British were denied the GTI G60. The reason given was that the MQ gearbox used was too large for the ABS and brake master cylinder to be fitted once the steering wheel had been moved to the right.

There was another G-lader version of the Golf — 'one of my favourite projects,' according to Volkswagen Motorsport manager, Klaus-Peter Rosorius. The Golf G60 Limited was part five-door Golf, part Golf Syncro and part Rallye Golf. This time the 16-valve engine was used, which meant 210bhp, a top speed of 143mph, and the tag

The GTI's standard gearing was retained for the 16V, the only exception being a slightly lower top gear. Suspension was lowered by 10mm.

The British had to wait until early 1986 before the 16-valve GTI was shipped to the UK...

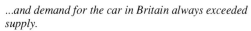

...and demand for the car in Britain always exceeded supply.

Two special equipment packages of the GTI and GTI 16V were introduced to celebrate the 10 millionth Golf in the summer of 1988. New alloy wheels, half-darkened rear-light clusters and three new metallic paint colours identified the cars externally. Inside, multi-colour striped upholstery, central locking and a Blaupunkt London or Atlanta radio/cassette player were featured. The costs were £10,987 for the GTI 3-door, £11,470 for the 5-door and £12,471 for the 16V.

of 'the fastest Golf to date'.

Only 70 were built, each virtually hand-made, which explains the cost of just under £24,000. The only real giveaways were the Volkswagen Motorsport badge and the brutish performance which lacked the civilised manners of a GTI.

The author, stuck in a London traffic jam in one of the cars, was hailed by a Ford Transit driver who was obviously a GTI buff. 'Not a normal 16-valve?' he queried knowledgeably. To which the only answer was that no, it was not!

More to the point, it was, quite rightly, not even known as a GTI. The limited production Rallye Golf and the G60 Limited had indicated that the GTI's reign as the ultimate Golf had come to an end. With the third generation and the advent of the volume production VR6, this was underlined.

By then, though, the GTI had assured itself a niche in automotive history. To be a trendsetter and remain at the top for so long was a tremendous achievement — the more so when one recalls its origins as an almost clandestine project for just a few enthusiastic test engineers.

The British press was unhappy that the GTI G60 was unavailable in right-hand-drive form. It was, after all, the ultimate mass-production manifestation of the Mk2.

The engine of the 130mph Rallye Golf was identical to that of the GTI G60, reduced to 1763cc to ensure that it remained in a lower motor sport category.

Nigel Walker, formerly Volkswagen Motorsport Manager but now with Audi, has described this Golf G60 Limited as his 'toy'. A Motorsport badge and blue grille are all that distinguish the 210bhp brute, of which just 70 were built.

4 The Tuners:
Beyond the Factory Standard

It all began with an advertisement, an ad. now famed in Golf GTI folklore. It was Sunday lunchtime at the home of Ray Potter, boss of Mocal oil control systems manufacturer and Aeroquip hose distributor, Think Automotive. Richard Lloyd, former Chevrolet Camaro and Opel Commodore racer, was glancing through the *Sunday Times* when he noticed it. The vehicle being offered was described as a unique, high-speed shopping car for the wife. In reality, it was a brand-new, silver, three-door, left-hand-drive GTI, supposedly the first in the country.

Lloyd, having already noted the model's performance in Germany, scraped together enough money to buy the car, and ran it on the road for a few weeks before deciding to 'sacrifice it as a competition car'.

It was a decision well made. At that stage the regulations for the then British Saloon Car Championship called for a 1600cc class. For three seasons, 1977-79, Lloyd was victor in that category. Further BSCC class victories were to result for the GTI with Demon Tweeks' Alan Minshaw in 1983 and James Shead in 1988.

Although, initially, Lloyd's car was prepared in 'spare time', it soon came to the attention of Volkswagen UK. With official backing, Lloyd was able to ask Broadspeed Engineering to look after the car. An employee of that famed race preparation company, Brian Ricketts, was given the responsibility.

Six races into the season, Ricketts enquired if a bill had been issued by Broadspeed. When it arrived, it amounted to Lloyd's total sponsorship money 'and a bit more'. Ricketts stated that, if Lloyd could find a building, he would run the car himself; thus was GTi Engineering conceived. The location was then, as now, Silverstone.

Track work inevitably led to road cars, with GTi Engineering initially converting about 33 to right-hand-drive. The first customer was Barry Treacy, then head of replacement wheel supplier, Wolfrace.

With the introduction of VW's own RHD model, GTi Engineering had to look further and subsequently developed a 1.8-litre version using Cosworth pistons and the crank from the American Rabbit. A few hundred of these conversions were carried out before VW came out with it own 1.8-litre model.

GTi Engineering was actually established in 1979, Lloyd with 51 percent of the shares, Ricketts with the remainder. A costly 1980, running Audi 80s in the British Saloon Car Championship, led to the company concentrating on road cars. When VW brought out its 1.8-litre version, 'the only thing we could do was to go bigger still'. A 2-litre conversion was therefore marketed. The company also became an agent for Oettinger, building its four-valve, 2-litre engines. (Scotts of Sloane Square is now the UK agent for Oettinger — oldest of the VW tuners — with all conversions now being carried out in Germany.)

Broadspeed took on Richard Lloyd's Golf in the wake of the Jaguar XJ5.3 failure. Driver Derek Bell is pictured here in the pits during testing in 1976.

GTi Engineering's Silverstone premises are deceptively modest. They are located on the perimeter road, just opposite Abbey Curve.

Above: Richard Lloyd's business was not only about GTIs, as this stand at the Racing Car Show indicates. Liqui Moly sponsorship of the RLR Porsche 962 showed that, for a while, GTi Engineering was the UK distributor for the German company's oil additives.

Right: Richard Lloyd's empire, while founded on the Golf GTI, also extended to the World Sports Car Championship. His Porsche 956 (pictured here at Monza) and 962 both proved race-winners.

Above: The Golf GTI 16V RE2100 Club Sport, the fastest GTi conversion, but perhaps not a typical example of the tuner's art. The company increased the capacity to 2.1 litres, modified the camshafts, manifolds and injection systems and upped the power to 190bhp.

Above: All laid out for one of GTi Engineering's famed engine conversions.

Left: GTI owners can get a head by going to BR Motorsport's Leamington Spa base.

In 1982 GTi Engineering was back on the race tracks with a Porsche 924, a project which led to GTi Engineering being separated from the motor sport, Richard Lloyd racing being established to handle that side of the business. The latter was to go on to run race-winning Group C Porsche 956s and 962s in the World Sports Car Championship.

GTi Engineering Limited (as opposed to Richard Lloyd Racing, t/a GTi Engineering) was formed — a name prohibited in the early days due to the existence of a company known as GT Engineering. Prior to 1985, Ricketts more or less ran the road side, while Lloyd concentrated on the racing.

In April of that year Ricketts had a very bad car accident which, ironically, involved a German tourist cornering on the wrong side of the road. A long period off work eventually resulted in the partners splitting, Ricketts leaving GTi Engineering to set up BRMotorsport.

With Ricketts' move, another former Broadspeed man, Dick Richards, took over as engineering director. The need for someone with conventional marketing skills was also recognised and Roger Abbey-Taylor, late of VAG and main dealers Dovercourt, was brought in as managing director. In the summer of 1991 the latter left the company, Lloyd himself taking back the managing role and former Audi man, David Ingram, joining the team to handle marketing.

On his arrival at GTi Engineering, it had seemed strange to Abbey-Taylor that the company was no longer involved in motor sport. Hence a return to the tracks, initially with Roger Jones winning outright the last Uniroyal Championship in 1989 using GTi Engineering's own GTI 16V. That was not the only 'pot' going around that year, Volkswagen Audi presenting the company with its 'Best Use of Motor Sport PR by a Dealer' award. GTi Engineering has dealer status with the importer; it is, in fact, the only officially approved Audi Volkswagen conversion specialist in the UK.

Racing in 1990 was fairly low-key, but the year after the company was back in the Esso Group N

Examples of Brian Rickett's work outside the BR Motorsport workshop.

Championship, preparing the Listers of Coventry car for VW specialist, John Morris.

When talking about GTi Engineering's road conversions, Roger Abbey-Taylor was quick to point out that 'there is nothing wrong with the car out of the factory. You have to be conceited to think you can improve on it'.

GTi Engineering had passed a milestone in September 1987 when it carried out its one thousandth conversion. The car in question was a new GTI 16V, the occasion being marked with a champagne reception at which VAG's sales and marketing director, Peter Cover, while congratulating the company, pointed out that 'our cars go pretty well in the first place'.

That is something with which Brian Ricketts concurs. In its day the 1600cc Golf was far ahead of anything seen before, yet it was such a simple engine with virtually a minimum amount of moving parts. It was so good in standard form that it was a job to improve it. You could change the cam, maybe the exhaust system, gas-flow the head and you would probably only get a maximum of an extra 15bhp, still retaining driveability. That was why in the early days GTi Engineering went for bigger capacity conversions.

Today the firm's quest is to 'try to make the car more driveable in the UK'. The emphasis is on 'the

UK' where, as the company points out, driving conditions differ from those in Germany. In real terms, this means plenty of low down power, and a quickening of overtaking times in the 40 to 70mph bracket. 'That is where most people in this country want it.'

'We want to achieve that without losing the flexibility of the engine. We don't want to detract from any of the basically good characteristics of the car.'

Most popular of the conversions from GTi Engineering is the 170bhp 1996cc RE2000 for the 16-valve GTI engine. Tuft- rided crankshaft, specially machined cylinder- block with 82.0 bore, lead-indium heavy duty crankshaft bearings, alloy pistons with valve clear- ance cut-outs, gas-flowed cylinder-head and inlet and exhaust manifold, re-profiled inlet and exhaust valve seats, selected valve springs and modified camshaft timing, distributor and injection system all lead to a top speed of 133mph and acceleration to match. The fact that the 50-70mph time has been cut from 10.4 to 6.9 seconds and the 70 to 90mph time from 12.7 to 7.7 seconds has even led people to dare comparison with the cars out of Maranello.

For both the 8- and 16-valve GTI units, Plus Pacs are offered to those who enjoy 'frequent use of the gearbox'. The line-up also includes 1870cc

When this photo was taken, Eric Mitchell (right) had already owned three turbo-charged GTIs. No wonder Rally Equipe proprietor Paul Ratcliffe looks pleased.

VW dealership Windrush created this special Mk1 using a Turbo Technics package.

Above: The early Turbo Technics system for the Mk1 GTI was later re-engineered to give improved response and mechanically simpler layout.

Left: Out of the way! Following his success with turbocharging the Mk1, Turbo Technics' Geoff Kershaw turned his attention to its successor.

Above: Golfs seen at Club GTI meetings vary from standard, to mild, to wild. All, though, are treasured possessions.

Below: It was fitting that Kamei should have been among the first to offer aftermarket styling for the GTI Mk1.

Above: Spotted at the 1988 Automechanika trade show in Frankfurt: styling and wheels from one of Germany's finest, the Black Forest-based BBS Kraftfahrzeugtechnik AG.

Below: Zender, available in the UK through North London-based Euro Styling, is another of the leading German body stylists to transform the looks of the GTI.

Although perhaps best-known as a Beetle specialist, Autocavan handles VWs and Audis of all kinds and has been involved with the GTI for many years. MD Geoff Thomas raced this Modified Saloon in the early 1980s.

and 1996cc conversions for both engines, as well as a whole range of accessory and tuning parts from wheels to sports suspension kits, body styling to leather gearknobs.

The ultimate GTi conversion, the RE2100 Club Sport, moves away from the company's usual philosophy with what David Ingram likens to a 'classical performance conversion'. The car is quick, very quick, but with a lumpy tickover and a tendency to be fluffy at the bottom end, not always easy to drive. 'It's just about as far as you can go with this engine,' Ingram states.

The figures are impressive, and so is the price, for this is not a cheap conversion. The 2.1-litre engine has a peak power of 190bhp and 168lb/ft torque at 6000rpm. It uses heavy-duty lead indium main bearings, Scrick camshafts and autothermic slipper pistons; the flywheel is lightened and the head gas-flowed, giving a 10.25:1 compression ratio.

The majority of enthusiasts running GTi Engineering conversions tend to be professional people in their thirties. A notable exception, however, is a quick lady customer on the west coast of Scotland, a sprightly lady in her seventies who is said to 'frighten the life out of her main dealer'.

Brian Ricketts reckons that his customers at BRM can be divided into two main groups. The younger driver tends to want a quick car with the ultimate handling, but the bulk of customers, like those of GTi Engineering, are more likely to be professional people, such as doctors, dentists and solicitors, wanting a 'Q' car, quick, but as safe and understated as possible.

Ricketts recalls his initiation into the GTI. 'As far as I was concerned, Volkswagens had a funny

Hella, perhaps better known for alternative GTI grilles, also alters the car's rear appearance.

THE BODY STYLISTS.

The Golf GTI has always been one of the most popular targets for the body stylists. Its straightforward looks have been transformed by a host of wings, spoilers, side skirts, wheel arches and grilles. The annual Treffen (see chapter eleven) has been a notable show-ground for these conversions, which have ranged from the subtle to the outrageous.

Predictably, it is the German body kit manufacturers who have dominated the scene. The founder of Kamei, Karl Meier, was a Volkswagen employee in the 1940s — indeed, he set up Kamei to produce custom-made components for the Beetle. So it was not entirely surprising that his company should be responsible for totally changing the appearance of the Mk1 and Mk2 GTIs with its X1 kits. Although body styling appeared on the wane at the 1991 Frankfurt Motor Show, Kamei was among a few that put their stamp on the new Mk3.

Zurich-based Rinspeed — a company which even has its own interpretation of the late 1980s Porsche Speedster — has designed gull-wing doors for the GTI.

Zender and BBS — the latter selling through the Volkswagen importer in the UK — are among a host of other German concerns to offer styling for the GTI, while Hella tends to look to the front of the car with its popular replacement grilles. In the UK, Richard Grant Accessories has been the only one able to take on the Germans at their own game.

The body-styling business has grown increasingly sophisticated in its use of materials and of wind-tunnels to ensure that its products are more than just cosmetic. However, it is clearly becoming increasingly passé to laden a GTI with such adornments. By and large, and despite some of the fine examples of styling seen on these pages, the GTI owner of the 1990s has a tendency to want his or her car to look just as its manu- facturer decided it should look. No doubt that pleases Giorgetto Giugiaro, for whom the Golf's original shape was a justifiable source of pride.

Richard Grant Accessories, based in the Bedfordshire village of Eaton Bray, has proved that it is not essential to be German to produce body styling for the GTI. Shown here are the front spoiler for a Mk1 and rear spoiler for the Mk2.

Walter Treser and his Car

Walter Treser, formerly one of Audi's top engineers, started his own company to offer aftermarket products for VWs and Audis, including the Golf. His dream was to create his own sportscar, a mid-engined car using the GTI's 16-valve unit. Seen here the day before its official unveiling at the 1987 Frankfurt Show, the car was to have been involved in a one-make race series. Sadly, Treser's company fell into financial trouble and, despite frantic attempts to save it, the receivers had to be called in.

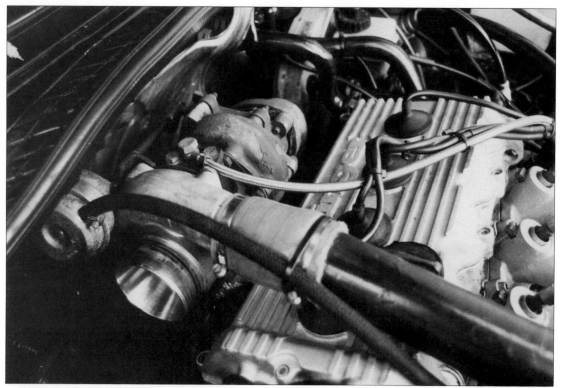

A "home-made" engine conversion on a Danish-owned Golf GTI. A pre-factory Oettinger 16-valve head is wedded to a Garrett turbocharger.

Outputs of 250bhp are not uncommon in Danish GTIs — nor are reliability and transmission problems.

noise in the boot.' His employer, Broadspeed, had been preparing the ill-starred works Jaguar XJ5.3Cs for the European Touring Car Championship. Those present at Silverstone for the 1977 Tourist Trophy could sense — despite the heroic performances of Tim Schenken, Andy Rouse and Derek Bell — that the end was at hand, not just for the 'Big Cats', but also, perhaps, for Broadspeed.

It was in the aftermath of the Jaguar episode that Ricketts was put to work on Lloyd's little Golf. 'I was staggered by the performance,' he remembers. At the time, Ford's famed BDA engine was producing 106bhp, yet this little hatchback was good for 110bhp.

Since then, Ricketts' fortunes have become so closely dependent on the car that he is now described in BRM's promotional material as 'one of the first in the country to recognise the vast tuning potential in the Golf GTI, and certainly the first to do anything about it'.

BRMotorsport actually got started in June 1987 with a 3,500-sq ft workshop in Leamington Spa.

By 1991, it was operating with eight full-time employees.

Its 8-valve conversions are, understandably, similar to those proven at GTi Engineering. The only difference is that, with the arrival of the 2-litre Volkswagen engine, instead of using an expensive forged crank BRM now uses the Passat 2-litre 16-valve.

'The nearer that you can stick to original equipment, the more reliable the engine conversion is going to be,' Ricketts states.

All the 16-valve conversions have been developed since the formation of BRM. With these, the company decided to give the customer a complete package which included free flow air cleaner and exhaust system. With the 8-valve conversions the engine and exhaust could be different from one car to another. 'With the 16-valve we went for the best driveability.'

All conversions have 'totally reliable' Schrick camshafts which Ricketts has been fitting ever since he first became involved with Golfs.

'I don't like mixing German engineering with British engineering as far as components are concerned because I feel that there is a difference in quality. People go and buy a Volkswagen because they want German engineering.'

Ricketts has tried to steer clear of turbochargers, but confesses to liking superchargers, having built such a Golf when he was at GTi Engineering. A phenomenal machine with 180bhp, 'it felt like driving a 5-litre,' he recalls. There is a possibility that he will turn his hand to supercharging the 16-valve Golf in the future.

BRMotorsport still often works on Mk1 cars, now rapidly becoming collectors' items. Many fine examples are still in existence. Customers might buy a car for around £3,000 and then spend another £5,000 on it because they do not like the newer shape. Several times BRM has taken the Mk1, fitted a BRM 152 2-litre engine, possibly a reconditioned gearbox with a higher cruising gear, and uprated the brakes with a BRM servo conversion.

BRMotorsport is an agent for Bilstein, Fichtel and Sachs and Boge shock absorbers. It also sells a certain amount of Koni product. Again, the company is going for German (or, in Koni's case, Dutch) engineering.

For the Mk1, Ricketts feels that Sachs, which supplies either an insert kit or a full strut kit, offers the best compromise between ride and handling. Bilstein, he reckons, will give the best handling, but tend to be too 'bumpy', especially for rear passengers. Being adjustable, Konis are in Ricketts' judgement fine for the GTI but again bumpier than Sachs.

One of the best improvements for the GTI Mk2 suspension is the Eibach anti-roll bar kit. 'I was just amazed, thinking that when you bolted this thing on it would understeer and then oversteer in the wet, but it literally transforms the handling.'

As the car goes into a corner the load goes on to the outside wheel because of the stiffer roll bar; the front dips and it pulls the other, offside wheel down on to the road, thus giving far better grip with no noticeable harshness in the suspension.

Club GTI chairman, David Pipes, also remarks how, after understeering around for eight years in various GTIs, an Eibach anti-roll bar kit brought neutral handling to his 16V.

On the firmer, lighter Mk1, the Eibach kit is excellent in the dry, but Ricketts reserves judgement on its performance in the wet, feeling that it tends to bring a little understeer.

Paul Bramford, managing director of Magard Limited, the UK distributor for Eibach, also handles Bilstein shock absorbers. He recalls that the Bilstein Golf GTI suspension kit was the first-ever damper and matched spring kit to be sold as a package for any car. It was developed by Volkswagen in conjunction with Bilstein. VW offered the marketing and distribution to the latter to sell through its worldwide outlets, rather than through Volkswagen dealerships.

In transforming the Golf Mk1's handling, the kit was the basis for a whole new industry.

Today Bilstein offers three kits. First came the BTS-0183, comprising complete struts, shocks and matched springs and giving a similar ride height to the standard car. This was followed by the BTS-0212, similar in setting and ride height to the first kit, but with inserts instead of complete struts, thus offering a cost saving. This latter kit is not suitable for 16-valve cars.

Following the dictates of the German market, a lowered version of the full kit, the BTS-0218, was introduced. Again it is recommended that this is not fitted to 16Vs, tyre clearance problems being possible due to their slightly heavier weight.

Such is Brian Ricketts' experience of the Golf GTI driver that he is able to sum up a customer and decide what best suits him or her. 'A customer can be a Sachs man, a Bilstein man or whatever...' The same applies to camshafts. Whether a wilder cam with a lumpy idle or the cam with a smooth idle is fitted tends to be decided on how Ricketts 'reads' the customer.

It was common to blame the cross-over linkage on the Mk1 for the poor braking performance. ('Even I was guilty of that,' Ricketts confesses.) At GTi Engineering the brakes conversion was to fit Mintex M171 performance pads which had been competition developed. Mintex first made these pads especially for the tuning company as they were not then available for the Golf. 'We even used to burn the old backing off standard VAG pads and send them to Mintex in Cleckheaton for the material to be fitted to the pads on the night-shift.' The

This is an advertisement.

PERFORMANCE
EXPERIENCE....
... QUALITY

These are the words for which AUTOCAVAN is famous. We have an unrivalled reputation for offering a full range of components to improve your GTI. When it comes to **performance**, we can offer throttle body kits, camshafts, adjustable camwheels and our renowned Powertorque exhaust systems — and plenty more. If it's **handling** you're after, then check the suspension kits from Sachs, Koni and our own **Autocavan** developed system. Take a look, too, at our anti-roll bars, suspension braces, Tarox brake kits and our SuperBrake system — all ready to transform your GTI. We also offer heavy-duty mountings for suspension, engine and transmission, as well as a full range of VDO instruments. Few companies can rival the **experience** gained by **Autocavan** in over **twenty years** of VW tuning. We were among the first to race a Golf in the UK, gaining valuable knowledge that we have been able to pass on to you. Remember, **there is no substitute for experience.** However, if there is one word above all others that **Autocavan** stands for it is **Quality.** We feel that your GTI deserves only the very best and our comprehensive range of components is unparalleled in terms of quality. We only market products that we know to be equal to, or better than, the OEM components. You can drive assured that, with **Autocavan** behind you, **your GTI will never have felt so good.**

AUTOCAVAN, 103 Lower Weybourne Lane, Badshot Lea, Farnham, Surrey
Telephone (0252) 333891 or Fax (02 2) 343363

Abt's grille treatment first seen at the 1991 Frankfurt Show for its Mk3 Golf 'Sportsline' harks back to its predecessor's round headlamps.

conversion grew so popular that Mintex subsequently brought out the application under normal production.

A stop was also fitted on the pedal and all the slackness taken out of the linkage. However, an early project at BRMotorsport concerned work on the Polo for VAG. A Polo servo-conversion predated the standard Polo servo first seen at the 1990 British International Motor Show. The Polo used the same rear brakes as a Golf Mk1 and the same diameter front brakes, which set Ricketts thinking that he could work similar magic on the GTI.

He looked for a better servo, for he felt that the GTI's servo was at fault. Initial tests were carried out which showed an improvement for the same amount of effort on the pedal from 940psi in the lines to 1450psi with the modified 3 to 1 ratio servo. This gave a much more progressive pedal and a lot less effort was required to make the brakes work.

The servos were modified at BRMotorsport using an AP type 38 3 to 1 servo converted to fit on to the Golf bracket and with a push-rod modification. A 13/16-inch diameter master cylinder is used, which gives slightly more fluid movement and helps to shorten the pedal travel.

This, says Ricketts, 'makes the car stop as it should'. Further improvement can be achieved with better pads or bigger discs. For the Mk1, it is possible to use 16-valve Scirocco Girling front callipers and 256mmx20mm, rather than 239mmx 20mm, discs. The greater diameter increases the radial torque and also helps dissipate the heat, as well as keep the pads more stable.

For road cars, BRM now favours the latest Ferodo non-asbestos pads which seem to have more bite than other non-asbestos material. Here British technology is used, as German materials, such as Pagid, tend to be harder-wearing but difficult to bed in, particularly if the discs are old.

The serious Golf GTI tuners in the UK are really few in number, with BRMotorsport and GTi Engineering perhaps the best known. Geoff Thomas' Autocavan is another which has been involved with the GTI since its early days, while Mark Yates' Mytech Engineering — another Leamington Spa-based concern — is a relative newcomer. The Mk1 GTI is still many people's favourite, but owners do not usually have vast sums of money to spend. For them, Tim Stiles Racing, in the Somerset town of Bridgwater, has developed a reputation for relatively low prices and indecently fast conversions. Even so, the company is now starting to carry out more work on 16Vs.

Stiles is a former schoolteacher whose Golf hillclimbing and racing activities indicated to him that an opening existed for the supplying of one-off engine conversions and performance parts. He had been racing Minis when he discovered Volkswagen, his Jetta GLi tow-car having been pressed into competitive action following a problem with the Mini.

Like BRMotorsport and GTi Engineering, Tim Stiles Racing has found customers among participants in the Slick 50 road saloon race series — a true test of the GTI, as will be seen in the next chapter.

A well-recorded example of Stiles' art has been his much-used X-registered demonstrator, a high-mileage Mk1 said to be more powerful than a modern 16V. Its obviously elderly and very standard looks belie a car which is half a second faster than the 16V to 60mph and a full four seconds faster between 40 and 80mph.

The heart of the car is TSR's 'C' pack head which has been polished and ported with 3mm exhaust and 40mm inlet enlarged valves, heavy-duty springs, guides and seals and a Piper 285 cam. The inlet manifold is matched to a big throttle valve. A large baffled sump and high compression pistons, modified from a non-injection Golf, are used.

The specification also includes a Boge suspension kit and Eibach anti-roll bar, while Mintex M171 brake-pads are the only change to the MK1's normally derided braking system. The basically road car's other life as a sprint and hillclimb machine is indicated by the Quaife limited-slip diff.

In Germany, the tuners' numbers are legion, with Oettinger and Abt Tuning being perhaps the most obvious. The former was responsible in 1977 for presenting the first prototype 16-valve GTI engine.

When it comes to turbocharging a Golf GTI engine, and not just Volkswagen engines, the UK turbocharging scene is headed by 'guru' Geoff Kershaw and his Northampton-based Turbo Technics operation. Both Janspeed and Turbo Technics encountered early problems in turbocharging the GTI. However, the latter overcame these, leading to one of its more popular conversions.

The Mitchell family from near Huddersfield, Yorkshire, almost became famous for being regular customers! In 1984 Turbo Technics dealer, Rally Equipe of Bury, was boasting that it had just carried out a conversion to retired production manager Eric Mitchell's 1800cc model, giving it a 0-60mph time of just under seven seconds and '30 percent more performance'. It made Mr Mitchell the first person in the country to have purchased three GTI conversions, his first having been a 1.6-litre model. It was not the last that his family was to buy.

Most recent of the TT conversions has been a 180bhp package for the 16V model. This gives 33 percent more power and a massive 53 percent increase in torque. Use is made of a Garrett T25 water-cooled turbocharger, incorporating two-stage boost control. The latter allows the driver the option of 0.40 bar (140bhp) or 0.65 bar (180bhp) through a dash-mounted switch. The compression ratio is lowered from 10.0:1 to 8.5:1.

Also utilised is a special, high nickel content, cast-iron exhaust manifold, while extra fuelling requirements are met by a fifth fuel injector which adjusts to boost pressure, giving optimum mixture settings at all times. Turbo Technics' own digital control unit retards the ignition under boost via its own built-in ignition map. An uprated Sachs clutch is also featured.

The performance for such a vehicle includes 60mph from rest in 6.1 seconds and a top speed above 130mph. Most impressive is the engine flexibility, with 4.5 seconds for 50-70mph fifth gear acceleration. The standard car takes 9.9 seconds!

The Kamei-styled Golf Mk3 retains the production
car's headlamps but sports wheel arch extensions over
7 1/2x17in wheels with ultra-low profile tyres.

Salvador Valiente, consistent winner of the Slick 50 Road Saloon Championship, campaigned first a Mk1, then (as pictured here) a Mk2. It is doubtful if anyone has won so many races behind the wheel of a GTI.

5 Circuit Racing: Domination of the National Scene

Arguably, the 'winningest' of all VW Golf GTI racing drivers has been London fruit importer Salvador Valiente, who only started competing when in his late 30s. During the latter half of the 1980s he won exactly half of his 80 races, and that figure becomes all the more impressive when one takes away 1985, his 'learning year'. During the next five years, he was victorious in 40 out of 64 events.

To this tally can be added 32 fastest laps and 22 pole positions. Valiente finished every race entered and spun only once, rotating at the Gooseneck on the picturesque Lincolnshire circuit, Cadwell Park, before going on to finish second.

We have already seen how Richard Lloyd first made the GTI into a racing car. It was watching Lloyd that attracted Valiente to the Golf, and it was to the former pop music manager that he took his engine to be prepared before the 1986 season.

The previous year he had merely fitted a roll-cage to his W-registered 1.6-litre Mk1 and gone racing. For Valiente's chosen class was the Road Saloons, brainchild of VW Scirocco driver Tim Dodwell, which insists that all competing cars are driven to, and from, the circuit. This particular category has shown all too well the tremendous race-potential of even the street-legal GTI: one of its greatest strengths has been that its performance and handling make it suitable for mild competition straight from the factory.

For Valiente's second season of racing, GTi Engineering breathed on his engine within the regulations, fitting a Schrick camshaft, Mahle pistons, and taking it out to 1781cc. The result was 137bhp, not as much as the 160-165bhp also to be found in the Road Saloon paddock, but enough to make the GTI competitive, nevertheless.

Valiente retained the black Mk1 throughout the 1987 and 1988 seasons, replacing it for the following two years with a 165-167bhp red Mk2. He found the balance of the heavier car tidier and reported that, while the Mk1s were prone to lifting rear wheels, the Mk2 'goes on rails'. But his heart remains with the Mk1. 'It was less predictable, but far more exciting. The Mk2 is more a family car; the Mk1 was a toy.'

1988 was particularly successful. Valiente stormed to victory in all 12 rounds of the championship, which was now sponsored by the engine and gearbox additive supplier, Slick 50. The previous year GTIs, usually Valiente's, had won every round but one — and that was taken by a Scirocco. As Brian Ricketts was later to comment, the championship could have been taken for a Formula GTI. Ricketts now muses on the potential of a series just for road-going GTIs and wonders if such an idea could become reality.

Those Slick 50 Championship GTIs were raced by a body of men so diverse that they ranged from a young heating engineer to the Chairman of the Royal Philharmonic Orchestra! The latter, one of the world's top french horn players, Jeff Bryant, bought Valiente's Mk1 for the 1989 season.

The Slick 50 Championship attracts a wide body of professions. Jeff Bryant is chairman and principal french horn player of the Royal Philharmonic Orchestra. He raced this ex-Valiente Mk1 in 1989, whenever commitments allowed. Bryant also uses a GTI as everyday road transport.

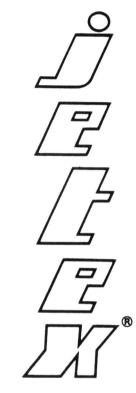

Valiente had been reluctant to let the car go and was perhaps only prepared to sell it to Bryant because he knew that orchestral duties would never let Bryant contest the entire championship!

The handling was not initially to Bryant's liking. He had raced an Alfasud, and it is said that Alfa drivers tend to find the transition difficult. 'Salvador liked to go round with the rear wheel a foot off the ground. It made me feel unsafe,' Bryant complained; but then it was a Mk1.

The car had originally been set up by Vic Lee to understeer. By changing Valiente's soft springs and firm damping for stiffer Leda springs and less damping, Bryant created a car which would tuck in when lifted off.

1989 brought serious challenges to Valiente's supremacy, first from the GTI of David Richardson — eventually to become champion in 1991 — and then, just to prove there were other cars out there too, from the Astra GTE of Mike Devine. Until he wrote the car off late in the season, it even looked as though the Oxfordshire driver might wrest the title from the Golfs. However, it has to be pointed out that Devine was running a Golf GTI as his road car and was to go on to race an Automotive Developments GTI in the production championships.

The next year Valiente met his match — by just one point — in the shape of newcomer Danny Bellamy. The latter's car, previously used for hillclimbing, was a MK1 GTI so elderly that it had already covered about 150,000 miles. It will come as no surprise to learn that Brian Ricketts had worked on the engine.

That Ricketts should be responsible for the engine of the winning road saloon in 1990 underlines the man's influence on the GTI's racing history. It was he, as we have seen, who prepared Richard Lloyd's Golfs. Once Lloyd's performance in his initially standard Golf had come to the notice of the importer, and VW's then UK competitions manager Jan Bannochie (now Jan Robertson) had given it official blessing, Lloyd was able to afford professional assistance and along came Ricketts.

Above: The Slick 50 crowd went abroad to race at Zandvoort in 1989. For once, the entrants did not have to drive their cars to the circuit. Most of the front running GTIs did not make the trip; those that did battled hard, but unusually were beaten by an Escort XR3i.

Below: Richard Lloyd, first to spot the racing potential of the GTI, seen here exiting Silverstone's Woodcote corner during a 1978 British Saloon Car Championship round. Lloyd had once worked in pop music with Cliff Richard's manager.

Lloyd's British success has been recorded in the previous chapter. He was also able to raise the GTI standard abroad. In the European Touring Car Championship race at Zolder in 1978, Lloyd and Belgian co-driver Teddy Pilette led the previously all-conquering Sciroccos in the Group 1 Golf. This, as was noted in that year's *Autocourse* annual, 'might well be a pointer for 1979'. The GTI, however, despite future class wins in the ETC, was to become more of a national than international star, with such as the Golf GTI Cup in Europe and domination of its relevant categories in the UK and (as described in chapter seven) the USA. The Golf GTI cup ran in Germany from 1977 to 1982, when it was replaced by the Polo Cup. Heinz Peil and Alfons Hohenester took two championships apiece during this period. In South Africa, Jochen Mass and Sarel Van Der Merwe raced a showroom-specification car to outright victory in the Castrol Six Hours.

Lloyd and Ricketts built up another GTI — a true Group 2 machine, motivated by a 187bhp Muller Tuning Engine — initially for use in the 1978 Tourist Trophy where the co-driver rolled the car in practice. The following year, with sponsorship from audio and video equipment manufacturer Akai, the team took in a number of ETC rounds. At the Brno Grand Prix in Czecho-slovakia, Lloyd and Swiss garage owner Anton Stocker scored the Golf's first class win in the series, finishing fifth overall in front of 120,000 onlookers.

At the Nürburgring a Scot by the name of Tom Walkinshaw made his front-wheel-drive racing debut as Lloyd's co-driver. It passed almost un-noticed, the fame he was to achieve as Jaguar's racing supremo being yet to come. What really excited the press was that Barry Sheene, 1976 and 1977 500cc World Motorcycle Racing Champion, made his car racing debut in the Golf at that year's Tourist Trophy. The car was fastest in its class that day, but was plagued by bad luck.

Found when perusing the press advertisements one Sunday lunchtime, Lloyd's original left-hand-drive GTI passed into the hands of Louis Parsons and Martin Grant-Peterkin.

Austrian Klaus Peter Rosorius, boss of Volkswagen Motorsport. At the Hannover premises, work is carried out on such as this Rallye Golf.

Golf GTI Mk1. Begun as an unofficial project by VW test engineers, the concept inspired little confidence among the company's sales personnel. (Author)

Old Mk1s never die, but they do sometimes have to be rebuilt. Kevin Nuttall created this colourful example from a write-off. (Author)

Left: Tim Stiles' high-mileage Mk1 is said to be more powerful than a modern 16V. Club GTI Chairman David Pipes (left) stands back as Tim takes this example of the tuner's art out on the track at Curborough. (Author)

Opposite: The Mk2 car was launched early in 1984, by which time competition from other manufacturers was fierce. However, it remained the leader in its class. (Author)

Right: The appeal of the GTI recognises no national barriers. This one was sighted in the fishing-port of Cameret, Britanny. (Author)

Below: Mytech Engineering is one of the many specialists to have worked on the Mk2. Racing driver Karl Hopkins enjoys the extra performance of the Mytech demonstrator. (Author)

Left: Pictured here in a rare English snow scene, the 16-valve Mk2 suffered from production delays but became available late 1985. It offered a strong increase in power over the 8-valve version and road testers compared it favourably with its rivals. (Author)

Below: Appearance of the much-refined Mk3 at the 1991 Frankfurt Motor Show aroused wide approval, though disappointment was expressed at the initial absence of a 16-valve version. (Author)

Right: Although the USA and South Africa already enjoyed 2-litre versions of the GTI, Europeans had to wait until the launch of the Mk3. (Author)

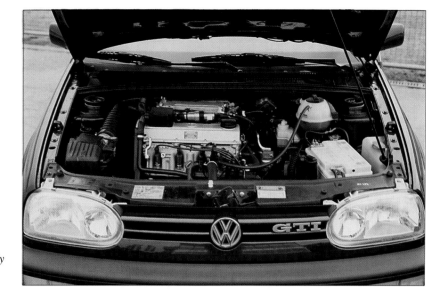

Below: With the introduction of the astonishingly fast VR6, Volkswagen kept its lead in the hot hatch race. Powered by a 2.8-litre engine, it has been called a "mini-Mercedes" (Author)

Left: Richard Lloyd's 1979 Championship-winning GTI passed into the hands of John Morris, stalwart of VW racing. This shot shows Morris at Thruxton in 1982. (Volkswagen)

Left: Demon Tweeks proprietor Alan Minshaw, seen here lifting a wheel at Silverstone, was a British Championship class winner in 1983. (Author)

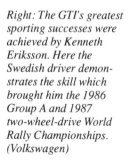

Right: The GTI's greatest sporting successes were achieved by Kenneth Eriksson. Here the Swedish driver demonstrates the skill which brought him the 1986 Group A and 1987 two-wheel-drive World Rally Championships. (Volkswagen)

Above: GTI USA. Santa Barbara provides the perfect backdrop for this 1991 Mexican-built 2-litre model. (Author)

Below: The Volkswagen stand at the 1991 Los Angeles Motor Show. GTI in foreground extols the virtues of Fahrvergnügen. (Author)

Left: Organised from Volkswagen's Milton Keynes offices, the GTI Driving Course gives owners the chance to learn from top instructors. Oulton Park is one of the four venues used. (Volkswagen)

Left: By far the biggest GTI event is the annual Treffen, held in the Austrian village of Maria Wörth. Enthusiasts from all countries attend, many with cars that are far from standard. (John Rettie)

Below: Graham Whittaker and Vicky Ellison have gone to enormous lengths to ensure that VAE 167 is one of the most highly-modified GTIs in Britain. Both are leading lights in Club GTI. (Author)

John Morris, who seems to have raced little else but VWs for years, took over Lloyd's mantle in the UK for 1981 and 1982, having bought the 1979 British championship car with Volkswagen's assistance. (The original 1977 GTI had gone to Louis Parsons and Martin Grant-Peterkin.) Morris' engine was built then, as now, by Neil Walker, an engineer with John Judd Engine Developments. Although the unit developed 148bhp, around 30 percent more than standard, it had difficulty in keeping up with the class-winning Toyota Corollas.

Morris returned to Sciroccos for 1983 and 1984, had a brief flirtation with the Ford marque, and was then back in a Golf for production racing in 1987. Ten years on from his first season in such a car, he was still racing one successfully in the Esso Saloon Car Championship, a series introduced in 1990 to be the pinnacle of production racing in the UK, a full Group N series just one rung below the Group A championship. In the interim, Morris had won the 1988 Uniroyal Championship and made a brief return to the British Touring Car Championship the following year.

(Coincidentally, Morris' 100th race at the wheel of a Volkswagen was at the GTI's tenth anniversary meeting on August Bank Holiday 1986.)

The change in British Saloon Car Championship regulations to Group A for 1983 brought about a little more restriction on engine modifications but more freedom on suspension. The GTI had to retain its Bosch K-Jetronic fuel injection, but more parts were becoming available from VW Motorsport in Hannover.

The British championship class title returned to the Golf that year. And not just to any old Golf, either. Cheshire performance retailer Alan Minshaw had bought Morris' now re-shelled ex-Lloyd GTI at the Racing Car Show. Like Salvador Valiente, the Demon Tweeks proprietor had been fired by Richard Lloyd's exploits, having started racing GTIs in 1981. His 'new' car had a Ricketts-prepared engine which was giving out 160bhp. A Schrick camshaft, Cosworth pistons and a 12:1 compression ratio all assisted.

Minshaw was the only driver to score points in all 11 races that year, thus further underlining the reliability of the racing GTI.

His next car was a Mk2, built up for him by Andy Rouse. It was not particularly competitive. The arrival of the 1.8-litre engine also brought a temporary setback for the GTI in the premier British saloon series, for it meant that the car had to compete in a 2.5-litre class. By 1985 the Golf was no longer in contention in the British championship, although 1.6-litre versions were still scoring class wins in the European series. While only one point was scored all year in Britain (by Minshaw), the Spanish driver Jordi Ripoles took three victories in Europe, including Class 1 in the Spa 24-Hours.

Minshaw continued to race Golfs in a variety of series, also entering James Kaye in the Uniroyal Production Championship in 1987 as well as a GTI in the 1988 British Touring Car Championship which was raced by Kaye, John Brindley and Minshaw himself. Slick 50 again appears in the story, this time as sponsor of Minshaw's 1988 team.

Minshaw is sure that he must have raced a GTI over 100 times, substantiating his opinion that 'it's just a wonderful car to drive'.

In 1987 the class break in the British Touring Car Championship was dropped to 2-litres, bringing the GTI back into contention. A year later, two of them vied for Class C honours; the final round, at Silverstone, saw James Shead and Andrew Jeffrey in with an equal chance, though one would have thought from the action that ensued that neither of them wanted the title. The fan belt snapped on Jeffrey's GTI, while Shead prayed his car to the finish with all the gauges right off the clock. Former champion Alan Minshaw proved an easy class winner that day.

The category in which the 1.8-litre Golf GTI has really excelled has been production racing, initial success coming with John Llewelyn's win in the 1983 Uniroyal Production Saloon Championship. True production racing boomed in the second half of the 1980s, only to decline in the early 1990s in favour of the full Group N Esso Superlube series.

GTIs abounded in such racing. During the period 1987-1990, the relevant class of the two production car championships fell every time to the Golf — eight out of eight class championships in four years! Production racing also gave the GTI

Above: GTI racer Alan Minshaw was 1600cc British Champion in 1983. Here he has obviously given commentator Ian Titchmarsh something to shout about.

Left: Golf GTIs versus Peugeot 205GTis at Brands Hatch in 1986. Jeremy Rossiter, director of Spax shock absorbers, ensures the Volkswagens are first into Paddock Bend.

Above: Yorkshireman James Kaye takes yet another Uniroyal Championship win at Brands Hatch in the Windrush/Demon Tweeks GTI.

Below: Brian Cox obligingly waving two wheels to the crowd in front of the Championship sponsor's banner. Cox turned in the fastest lap in class during this 1989 August Bank Holiday Firestone round at Thruxton.

*Young Karl Hopkins arrived from motocross to take
the Firestone Championship by storm in 1989, his first
year of car racing.*

the chance to show its capabilities in 24-hour races, the Willhire 24-hour event at Snetterton being run for this category.

Contrary to the various previews (and at least one national magazine's report of the event!), Simon Davison did not take part in the 1987 Willhire race. The RAC refused to grant Volkswagen's rally star a licence, due to his lack of circuit racing experience. He was thus unable to share the troubled Whitehouse GTI of Vic Lee, Jeremy Rossiter and Gary Ayles, which managed only sixth in class. But GTIs also came first, third and fourth in class, led home by the Listers of Coventry car of John Morris, Bob Meacham and Barrie Williams.

The following year, as the Sierra Cosworths fell by the wayside, so the Golf GTIs moved up. Roger Jones and Paul Taft battled with Nick Baughn and Rob Kirby for class leadership. However, the pace of the early hours caused the former pair to lose a couple of laps in the pits, a disadvantage they were unable to overcome. The Northway Garage car of

Baughn and Kirby eventually finished third overall behind a Cosworth and a BMW M3, while the Jones/Taft pairing came sixth. Fourth and fifth places in Class C also fell to Golf GTIs.

One of the 'long-distance' Uniroyal races in 1987 saw motoring PR man Gordon Bruce sharing James Kaye's Windrush Motors/Demon Tweeks car, the pair finishing a creditable second behind Vic Lee. Ironically, it was 12 years since Bruce, then road test editor of *Motor*, had appeared in a full-page national advertisement stating that the Golf was 'not really my sort of car'. It should be added, though, that by the end of the innovative advertising campaign, his attitude had softened. He has even been known since then to run a GTI as his personal transport.

Kaye won Class C of the Uniroyal series that year. Having started the season at the wheel of a Honda Civic, the Yorkshireman had soon moved over to a Golf, immediately winning his class on four consecutive occasions. Vic Lee, then general manager of Dartford VW dealer Whitehouse, later

better known as an entrant in one of the top BMW M3 teams in the British Touring Car Championship, took the other series, then sponsored by Monroe shock absorbers.

Nigel Walker, Volkswagen UK competitions manager at the time, reckons that Lee's Quantum-backed GTI was 'the start of professionalism in production racing'.

For participation in production racing, a standard GTI 16-valve would be taken and luxuries such as the sunroof, tinted and electric windows removed. A full roll-cage, fire-extinguisher and ignition cut-out switches would be fitted, as well as a 3.5Kg Kevlar racing seat and four-point harness. By blueprinting, power could be improved from 139 to 175bhp. Although shock absorbers had to remain standard, the damping could at least be uprated.

At the start of the 1988 season Volkswagen Motorsport announced that, although it was no longer running its Junior Rally Team, it was still actively encouraging Golf GTI drivers with a

boosted bonus programme. By the time the season began, 15 GTI and GTI 16V drivers had entered for the rally programme, while 17 had signed up for the racing programme which encompassed the Uniroyal, Monroe and premier, now Dunlop-sponsored, British Group A series.

Roger Jones, managing director of Silver Shield Automotive Glazing, took the Uniroyal Championship outright that year in GTi Engineering's 16V, having won his class on 12 out of 14 occasions. According to Roger Abbey-Taylor, then GTi Engineering's MD, 'we went into production saloon car racing to prove that we could run a team successfully'. It would seem they succeeded.

A year later, Jones was out in the new Esso Saloon Car Championship. Using a GTI prepared by 7 to 12 Autos of Milton Keynes he was again successful, taking Class C of the series. Former moto-crosser Karl Hopkins took the equivalent class in the Firestone (formerly Monroe) series, in only his first season of racing. The GTI had swept the Class C production board for four seasons.

1991 Le Mans winner Johnny Herbert was one of those who used the Golf GTI-based engine to win the British Formula Three Championship.

Behind Formula Three

The Stuttgart engine tuner Siegfried Spiess was the first to convert a Golf GTI engine for use in Formula Three single-seater racing, German driver Harald Henzler winning the opening event of the 1979 season with the unit.

Dave Scott was the first to use GTI power — a John Judd unit — to win a round of the British Formula Three Championship, coming home first at Brands Hatch in August 1982. The 170bhp VW engine used in F3 is, in fact, an enlarged 2-litre version of the light and slim unit found in the 8-valve Golf. The required 23mm restrictor in the inlet manifold evens out the difference between an 8- and 16-valve engine.

The championship fell to a Volkswagen driver for the first time in 1984, when Scotland's Johnny Dumfries took the spoils. Subsequently, Mauricio Gugelmin, Andy Wallace, Johnny Herbert and David Brabham all used the GTI engine to take the series. Dumfries, Wallace and Herbert were also to have in common the achievement of winning at Le Mans. Brabham, Gugelmin, Dumfries and Herbert were all to taste Grand Prix racing.

In the UK the GTI engine had notched up 60 consecutive wins by mid-1987, Johnny Herbert using a Spiess unit to record the milestone. After that, Toyota, Alfa Romeo and Honda power began to challenge VW's domination, ending what had become a run of 63 straight victories. In its native Germany, however, the engine remained dominant; indeed, Klaus-Peter Rosorius, Volkswagen Motorsport Manager, has described the period as having been 'too successful'. The Volkswagen Board wondered why it was no longer receiving publicity from Formula Three! Still, Rosorius was able to smile as he referred to the category as 'Formula Super VW'.

Despite the competition, and thanks to tuners such as John Judd and Siegfried Spiess, the GTI-based engine continued to win rounds of the British F3 Championship. The 80th victory was achieved at Thruxton on May 27 1991 by another Briton, Steve Robertson, in a Bowman Racing Ralt-Spiess RT35. The GTI unit is still, according to Bowman team owner Steve Hollman, 'the right choice'.

Kalle Grundel kicks up the 1983 dust with this Group A GTI. The Swede had reached his mid-thirties before he attracted attention driving for the Volkswagen works team.

6 Rallying: Golf GTIs in the Rough

Steve Davies, Volkswagen Junior Rally team member, arrived at the Ambleside service halt and tentatively proposed that he take over the driving of Simon Davison's Golf GTI. It had been suggested that the four members of the team all looked so alike that nobody would notice the difference.

Despite a splitting headache, worsened by a vibration from the sump guard, Davison would have none of it. His works drive, here on the 1986 Lombard RAC Rally, was the reward for being the most successful member of the Junior team during the season (in which he had won the Group A class of the National Rally Championship). Still, there were elements of the rest of the team in the entry. Davies' regular co-driver, Nicky Grist, was reading out the instructions, while the car was that used throughout the season by Scottish team member, Callum Guy. Only the Irish element was missing.

All year the quartet, the Englishman, the Welshman, the Scot and the Irishman, Robin Phillips, had worked towards this end; and now the winner, despite his adversities, was proving capable of competing with the world's best. On the final day of the rally Davison was matching, or even bettering, the stage times set by his illustrious 'team mate', the Hannover works entered Kenneth Eriksson. And, unlike the Northumbrian, Eriksson had a 16-valve engine; indeed, had had use of one since the 1000 Lakes Rally.

For the Swede, in his 193hp Triumph Adler-sponsored Golf GTI, there was more at stake.

Already the world record-holder for driving a car on two wheels, he was on course to clinch the Golf's first World Championship. 1986 was the last year of the spectacular Group B rally cars. The following season, the world series was to be for the gentler Group A. However, it had been decided that the latter would have their own World Championship just for 1986, and it was this that the boyish-faced Eriksson was leading.

A temporary halt in a water-splash on day one meant that he was only in third spot. Problems with Lasse Lampi's Audi Coupe enabled him to pull back into second. However, Ingvar Carlsson's Mazda 323 was still ahead when the cars returned to Bath. Eriksson had failed to repeat Kalle Grundel's Group A win of three years previously, but he had secured the championship for Volkswagen and the Golf GTI.

Prior to the RAC Rally, Eriksson had won the Group A categories of the New Zealand, Argentine and San Remo Rallies, his best overall results being fifth on the last two. Throughout the season he had been partnered by the experienced Peter Diekmann who, for the previous couple of years, had sat next to Kalle Grundel.

Grundel, a Swede, had appeared on the scene as a works driver in the early 1980s, having taken a self-prepared GTI to fifth overall on the Swedish Rally. His arrival coincided with the introduction of the production-based Group A category, as well as a 160bhp 1800cc engine. With such, he took on

Sachs
Originals...

...Impossible
to copy.

Above: Kenneth Eriksson tells Volkswagen Audi PR man Edward Rowe of the perils of the Sutton Park special stage. The Swede was to go on to secure the World Rally Championship for Group A on the 1986 RAC Rally.

Below: Eriksson's Two-Wheel-Drive Championship-winning GTI was displayed at the 1987 Frankfurt Motor Show. Eriksson was overall winner that year on the Ivory Coast Rally and gave Audi a fright on the Safari.

Jochi Kleint (above),
Erwin Weber (far right)
and Simon Davison (right)
take to the air in their Golfs.

Volkswagen Junior Team Member Steve Davies presses on during the 1987 Fram Welsh International Rally. Margam Park is the scenic location.

the Group B supercars on the 1983 RAC Rally, finishing eighth overall and dominating Group A.

1984 saw regular entries in the World Championship and the introduction of the less nervous Mk2, which made its debut on the 1000 Lakes Rally that August. That year, Grundel and Diekmann won the Group A categories of the Portugese — by over 40 minutes — and San Remo — despite rolling on the first stage — championship rounds. The influential *Rallycourse* annual placed Grundel among its top 10 drivers, thanks to 'giant-killing performances for VW in the GpA Volkswagen Golf'. The annual was not alone, though, in pointing out that Grundel, now well into his thirties, was no youngster.

VW Motorsport had now experienced a couple of low-budget seasons supporting the World Championship, but it was only with the chance of the one-off FIA Cup for Group A in 1986 that it took on a season-long challenge. Its success on that with Eriksson gave it the confidence to enter a two-car team for the following year, with German,

Erwin Weber, joining the young Swede at the wheel of the 16-valve GTIs.

Group A was the making of Eriksson, his driving of the works Golf that year being the stuff of which rallying legends are made. His second place in New Zealand and his fourth in Argentina could be singled out. His reward came with outright victory on the Ivory Coast Rally.

He led from the start, although his victory was soured by the aeroplane crash which took the lives of Toyota Team Europe co-ordinator Henry Liddon, and of leading co-driver Nigel Harris. TTE withdrew from the rally, so it will never be known if Björn Waldegård's Supra Turbo would have caught the Golf. Still, this should not detract from Eriksson's victory. He drove faultlessly, troubled only by niggling transmission problems. The team did not have the resources of its Japanese rivals and all but one of its members had never seen the Ivory Coast before.

Not since the days of the Saab 99 had a front-wheel-drive car been a serious championship

Simon Davison, the most successful member of the 1986/7 Volkswagen Junior Rally Team.

Simon Davison exits the Knockhill rallycross circuit during the 1987 Scottish Rally.

Freed from the perhaps premature responsibility of a works drive, Callum Guy performed well in the 1987 Esso Scottish Rally Championship. Here he is seen on the Tudor Webasto Manx Rally.

contender. Overall, Eriksson finished fourth in the World Championship, while winning another one-off series, the two-wheel-drive championship.

Berliner Peter Diekmann was presented with the Halda Co-Driver of the Year Award, the jury citing how he and Eriksson had pushed their car four kilometres on the first stage of the Argentine Rally.

Eriksson's two championships were the pinnacle of success for the GTI in rallying, part of a story begun with 120bhp 1600cc-engined cars in what was then the production-based Group 1. The year 1978 saw VW Motorsport, led then as now by Klaus Peter Rosorius, introduce a 180bhp Group 2 version which Jochi Kleint used to good effect.

The car's first major win came in 1979 with Per Eklund, then a Saab works driver, taking it to victory on the Sachs-Baltic Rally. The following season Eklund finished fifth for the Hannover team on the Monte Carlo Rally, having run in the top three for most of the event. Further success in those early years came with victory in the 1981 German Rally Championship.

The final international fling for the GTI came in 1989. That year the factory cars did not display the amazing turn of speed they had shown in the two previous World Championship seasons. However, the car achieved its best result on a true classic event when former World Champion Stig Blomqvist brought his home to third on the Marlboro Safari Rally. The event, regarded as one of the roughest Safaris of all, had proved to be a test of survival, thanks to heavy, unseasonal, road-destroying rain.

On the national rallying scene, Golf GTIs inevitably became common in Germany, but it was only following Kalle Grundel's Group A win that British competitors saw the car's potential. The David Sutton-run Volkswagen Junior Team of 1986 gave the car a high profile.

The team was a £250,000 attempt by Volkswagen to 'find a new British rally star'. Following advertising, 350 applicants were whittled down to 30 to be interviewed. Simon Davison almost missed out when his application was lost in the post.

There is a story, perhaps apocryphal, that one of the interviewees — a version of the tale says Callum Guy — was asked if he would give up everything for his sport. The next question

The Volkswagen Junior Rally Team left a trail throughout 1986 and 1987. Broken stub axles proved an initial problem for the less experienced members.

Ludwig Dammiger and Rüdiger Kern were Volkswagen Motorsport's two drivers for the 1986 German Rally Championship, the Deutschen Rallyemeisterschaft.

requested the name of his favourite restaurant…

There was no doubting that Volkswagen wanted dedication from its team. The chosen four were clad in blazers and taught that even how they appeared at a prize-giving was an important part of the equation.

By the end of the season, Davison had taken the National Group A driver's title and Volkswagen the National Rally Championship Manufacturers' Award. Volkswagen's then UK marketing manager, John Meszaros, was moved to remark that 'it totally vindicates our decision to back Britain's up-and-coming rally stars. They have proved that they have what it takes to beat the best.'

The UK importer continued this programme into 1987 with Davison moving up to the British Open Championship and Steve Davies and Robin Phillips staying with the National series. Callum Guy was left to fund his own way, mainly in the Esso Scottish Championship. The removal of the premature responsibility of a works drive gave the young Scot a new lease of life.

Davison was one of the heroes of the Circuit of Ireland Rally that year. However, it was the GTI that he used for pace notes which made the news. Stolen by joyriders from outside his Belfast hotel, the car was discovered in the vicinity of Anderstown armed police station. The Army told the David Sutton mechanics that they were quite at liberty to try driving it first…

Unfortunately, by mid-season Volkswagen Motorsport decided to drop out of the Marlboro/*Autosport* National Championship, although Davies and Phillips were told they could still use their cars, provided they met the costs. Davison continued in the Shell Oils Open series, joined in a couple of the remaining rounds by either Davies or Phillips.

David Sutton-prepared GTIs were particularly popular that year. On the Tudor Webasto Manx Rally they numbered an unprecedented five. Davison and Davies were joined by the irrepressible Guy (who had backing from his employer, Equity and Law International), Tony Saddington and the Finn, Sebastian Lindholm. Lindholm had been a contender for the championship with his Audi Coupe but, unable to get it back into tarmac specification following the 1000 Lakes, he sought vital points with one of Sutton's 16-valves. Hordes of Group N 'showroom' GTIs also indicated the popularity of the car on the Continent, for this was a round of the European Championship.

Later in the year, Sutton's mechanics changed a gearbox on Eriksson's RAC Rally car in just 17 minutes 55 seconds — even faster than when they undertook a similar job for the BBC television programme, *Top Gear*.

Beetle specialist Francis Tuthill won the Group N 2-litre class on that RAC. The only replacement he required throughout the entire rally was one set of brake pads. It spoke volumes for David Sutton's preparation of the car, which had been purchased brand-new just a fortnight before.

The following year Andrew Wood, the taciturn Scot who had made his name at the wheel of GM machinery, put together a package to run a Sutton GTI 16V in the Open Championship while Simon Davison was retained by the importer for a third year. Sutton, though, was to split from Volkswagen Audi at the end of 1988. He had been running Audis for the importer, as well as Golfs, and it was the withdrawal of the former from British rallying, plus a meeting at Ingolstadt which confirmed that there was no competitive replacement likely 'for two or three years', that made him 'feel that I must look elsewhere'.

The next year, 1989, Volkswagen Motorsport UK decided to put its money into a bonus scheme for GTI competitors. As manager Nigel Walker pointed out: 'In rallying the Golf has demonstrated that it has the ability to take class titles and is a strong, easy car to maintain.'

It was a decade since GTIs had first taken to the rough in the UK, John Button's 240bhp, 16-valve, twin-overhead camshaft rallycross cars being among the pioneers. The car was to enjoy its share of rallycross success, the European Championship Division 1 category having fallen to Norwegian Egil Stenshagen twice in the early 1980s.

1989 also saw the introduction of the Golf Rallye G60 which, said Volkswagen optimistically, was 'designed to win the World Rallying

Halda Award-winning co-driver Peter Diekmann was an important figure in the development of the rallying GTIs, navigating for both Kalle Grundel and Kenneth Eriksson.

Championship'. The next year the 280bhp super-charged car appeared in competition, to be driven by such as Mark Lovell in Britain and Erwin Weber on the World trail. The latter has also used the G60 to good effect in his home country, dominating the German National Championship.

The G60 is not, strictly, a GTI. However, there is a chance that a GTI may yet return to top-level rallying; at least there will be if the matter is left to Herbert Schuster.

Talking at the launch of the third generation Golf, Schuster said: 'We are reflecting on how we want to continue in terms of "rally racing". No decision has yet been made, but we know that the six-cylinder, normally aspirated engine has less of a chance because the regulations give preference to turbocharged engines. We are considering the (yet to be introduced two-litre) 16V engine by fitting a G-lader, but nothing has been finally decided.

'Nowadays in rally racing you need a four-wheel-drive car. Without four-wheel-drive, you have no chance, but all of this costs a lot of money.'

So a future step *could* be a four- wheel-drive, G-lader, two-litre GTI 16V Mk3. But: 'I have no idea when this will happen. At the earliest it would be 1993 or '94, assuming decisions are made in time. Until then we will continue with the A2 Golf, testing new assemblies — engines, running gear and so on — in the older vehicle.'

Above: John Rettie's 1981 Golf GTI, federalised for use in the United States and distinguished by its 15in Ronal wheels and BFGoodrich Comp T/A Tyres.

Below: Rettie, a prime mover behind the introduction of the GTI into the United States, looks out from a 1991 two-litre model.

7 Superbunny:
The GTI in the USA

John Rettie was a European, an Englishman to be precise. As such, he could not understand Volkswagen's attitude to the Golf in the United States. It was not the fact that they called it a Rabbit, which to the European had undertones of a most timid driver. It was the fact that, years after the GTI had set new standards in Europe, it was still being ignored in America. The spiritual successor to the beloved Beetle seemed, if anything, to be the Rabbit Diesel. Rettie blamed Jane Fonda and her appearance in *The China Syndrome* for that.

Back in the early 1970s Volkswagen was still, far and away, the number one car importer in the United States. By 1975, however, the Beetle had all but died. The company had rested on its laurels — had failed to see the Japanese coming. Its new cars for the US, the Rabbit and Scirocco, also had reliability problems.

Despite this, the diesel version of that which the rest of the world called the Golf was fairly successful. The German manufacturer also set up its own US manufacturing plant in Westmoreland, Pennsylvania.

By the 1980s, VW had come to realise that what its customers wanted was a true Teutonic driving feel. As Volkswagen of America vice-president, Jim Fuller, tragically to be killed in the Lockerbie disaster, was to state, this was to cut it off from a large section of the US market. American motorists, Fuller used to reckon, could be divided into 'transportation people' and 'driving people',

the latter accounting for only twenty-five percent of the total. Volkswagens, he declared, appealed only to the 'driving people'.

Volkswagen's error had been to believe that it could appeal to the total market. It 'Americanised' its cars for the US public, thus alienating itself from the true driving enthusiasts, those who in Europe regarded the Golf GTI as a manifestation of the ultimate.

John Rettie had moved to California in 1975, swapping his position as assistant editor of *Safer* (later to become *VW) Motoring* for that of technical editor at *Hot VWs*. It was perhaps logical that, at the latter, he should concentrate on the water-cooled models. To his American colleagues, a Volkswagen was still a Beetle.

Rettie needed a Volkswagen he could believe in. In search of this, he modified a Rabbit to give a similar performance to a GTI. Fitted with side-draught Webers, as well as Bilstein shock absorbers, it could hardly be called a GTI. Rettie decided upon 'GTR', the R standing in theory for 'Rabbit', though perhaps in practice for 'Rettie'.

In 1981 he decided to go for the real thing and brought in a European Golf GTI through Luxembourg. His first task would hardly appear arduous to the GTI enthusiast. He had to put at least 5,000 miles on the clock in order to classify it officially as a used car. In the end, with a trip through Europe which included following the Acropolis Rally, he recorded nearer 7,500.

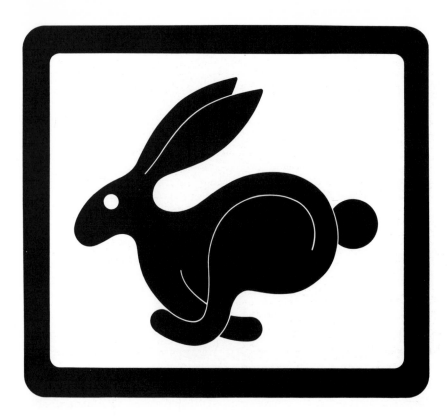

There was a time in Europe when the term 'rabbit' would have suggested the opposite of the average GTI driver! Nevertheless, it was the name used in America for all the early Golfs, including the GTIs. When the Evironmental Protection Agency released its 1975 fuel economy list, it also let the name of the new Volkswagen out of the bag... or should it be hat?

The next step was to federalise the car, a matter of fitting a catalytic converter, recalibrating the fuel ignition, fitting rear seat-belts — no problem, as the anchorage points were already in place — and fitting side repeater lights. The bumpers remained, but Rettie had to bolt on hydraulic rams from the Rabbit. It was, he recalls, 'fairly straight-forward'.

There may have been a few other Golf GTI's around in the United States — indeed, Rettie was soon to see a 'twin' in Newport Beach. However, thanks to a road test in the November 1981 issue of *Motor Trend*, his became the first in the public eye.

'Happiness,' extolled Jim McGraw, author of the article, 'is driving a truly capable car in a sea of plain vanilla… the GTI… is so light and nimble it allows the driver to humble a host of Goliaths like Corvettes, TR8s and Porsches — let alone the hordes of plain vanilla cars.' The GTI, he stated, was 'a factory hot rod, a classic example of parts-bin engineering applied to a proven platform.'

McGraw's enthusiasm took him almost over the top: 'the Golf GTI takes to a dragstrip like Brooke Shields to a camera, with similar magical results'.

Sadly, for all the excitement McGraw's readers

must have felt, the quickest Rabbit then available to them was the lacklustre Rabbit S. As McGraw pointed out, John Rettie was a British citizen for whom bringing in a GTI was easier. But the *Motor Trend* staff were not going to leave it like that. In the same issue, they penned an open letter to Volkswagen. The gist was that, with the GTI, the company had acquired a tremendous name, yet here in the United States it was missing the market. Surely such a car would revive Volkswagen's flagging fortunes in America? It should be an easy matter: the engine was, after all, fuel injected and would therefore meet US emission regulations.

'Introduction of a US GTI would be an in-expensive, yet effective, way of boosting the VW image in America,' the letter declared. 'So how about it, VWoA? Build us a Rabbit GTI and give Americans a reason to leave their Porsches at home.'

Within a week, a telephone call was received from no less a person than Jim Fuller. 'Loved your article and letter,' he stated; 'just wait one year.' Sure enough, one year later the first Rabbit GTI appeared as a 1983 model. It was six years since the car had first been seen in Europe.

Above: Not quite a GTI. The Americans had their own specification for the Golf which they called the Golf GT.

Below: Interior of a US 1988 Volkswagen GTI 16V. Note the Americans do not use the name 'Golf' for this model.

An Open Letter to VWoA

November 1981

Volkswagen of America
Englewood Cliffs, New Jersey

Dear VWoA:

Ten years ago in Europe the fortunes of Volkswagen
were in jeopardy. The Beetle was no longer the darling
of the car-buying public, and every new air-cooled VW
model (1500, 1600TL, 411, etc.) was a disaster. Then,
in 1975, partly due to your company's acquisition of
Audi, you were able to introduce two front-wheel-drive
water-cooled cars: the Golf and the Scirocco. Diehard
VW enthusiasts were horrified, but consumers felt that
you had at last built a "real automobile". Since then
the Golf and its American counterpart, the Rabbit,
have dominated the small-car scene. This is apparent
in the number of Golf/Rabbit clones that have sprung
up in Europe, Japan and the U.S.

The incredible success of the gasoline-powered Golf
GTI (more than a quarter of a million sold) proves
that there are enough people in Europe who still
desire both economy _and_ performance in one package.
These are people new to the VW family, people who
would never have owned a Beetle, considering it a car
primarily for those who couldn't afford more. The GTI
is an "in" car — everyday transportation for a car
lover who might also own a Porsche.

But Volkswagen of America seems interested in selling
economy only. True, last year you sold almost 100,000

_This is the full text of the open letter written by "Motor
Trend" to Volkswagen of America in November 1981.
Exactly a year later, the Rabbit GTI appeared as a
1983 model, to be greeted by enormous acclaim._

diesel Rabbits. But it is our opinion that many Americans want more from a small car than just economy and would welcome a small, high-performance gasoline-powered car. We don't subscribe to the notion that American car buyers are less demanding or sophisticated than the Europeans. So if the GTI is such a great success in Europe, why isn't it available in this country?

The U.S.-made Rabbit S is really a detuned version of the GTI with a larger displacement engine. Both use a fuel injection system. To equal the performance of a GTI, you would have to certify a new engine. Even if this cost you $250,000, and you sold only 20,000 cars, the cost of certification would add a mere $12.50 to the price of each car, an amount enthusiasts would gladly pay.

All the parts necessary to transform the Rabbit S into a genuine U.S. version of the GTI are off-the-shelf items that can be bolted on. In Europe, the GTI costs only $1,100 more than the Golf GLS. The Rabbit S lists here for $7,050; it would be easy for you to build a federalized GTI here and sell it for well under $10,000. Last year you sold nearly 9,000 Rabbit convertibles; there is no denying the demand for specialty Rabbits, even if they are expensive.

Introduction of a U.S. GTI would be an inexpensive, yet effective, way of boosting the VW image here in America.

So how about it, VWoA? Build us a Rabbit GTI and give Americans a reason to leave their Porsches at home.

Regards,

The Motor Trend Staff

The Motor Trend Staff

-2-

Above: America's 1991 Volkswagen GTI 16V. Two-litre models were available there a year before they could be had in Europe.

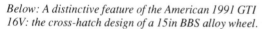

Below: A distinctive feature of the American 1991 GTI 16V: the cross-hatch design of a 15in BBS alloy wheel.

Exactly twelve months after the *Motor Trend* feature, *Car and Driver* carried an article sub-headed 'The car we've all been waiting for'. The magazine had its hands on a Westmoreland-built Rabbit GTI. 'One killer shoe-box,' it said.

The same month, *Road & Track* called the GTI 'the panacea for everything from the blues to the blahs'.

At the press launch, Duane Miller, Volkswagen of America's vice-president of engineering, explained that the initial idea had been to build a tamer vehicle, simply adding sports seats and 'GTI-like suspension' to the heavier Rabbit S. However, the improved handling only served to show up the relative lack of horsepower.

According to Miller, two 1981 events in Germany had made the Rabbit GTI possible. One was the introduction of 14-inch alloy wheels for the Quantum (as the Passat saloon was called in the USA) which would fit the Rabbit. The second was the decision to develop a federalised version of the 1983 Golf GTI's 1.8-litre engine. The more

*A two-litre GTI from Larry Brown's VW West Coast
press fleet poses in the hills just north of Los Angeles.*

powerful engine allied to the larger and wider wheels meant that the US engineers felt capable of going ahead with their own GTI.

As far as the American public is concerned, there has never been such an animal as the Golf GTI. Those early models followed the lead of the rest of the US line-up and were known as Rabbits. With the introduction of the second generation, all the Rabbits metamorphosed into Golfs... except the GTI. That simply became the 'GTI', without the Golf prefix. It later became the GTI 16V, but it has never been the Golf GTI in the United States.

Those early GTI's manufactured in Westmoreland were very close to their European counterparts in specification, though only good for 102hp, somewhat short of the German output. The cam from the stock 1.7-litre four-cylinder engine was retained in order to fatten up the midrange for better around-town response, an element lacking in the high-winding European GTI.

The Rabbit GTI was 140lbs heavier than the Golf GTI, and thus had to have its own suspension configuration in order to match the European handling as closely as possible. While the front MacPherson struts came from VW's European supplier, the rear shock absorbers were Sachs units.

At the launch press conference, the company predicted sales of 12,000 in the first year. The journalists present reckoned the little car to have a potential sale of 20,000. In the event, both parties were wrong. The final figure for the first complete year was 27,782.

Larry Brown, PR chief of Volkswagen's West Coast operations, recalls that he loaned one of just three prototypes to a photographer and then had the unenviable task of phoning head office in Troy, Michigan, to report that the car had been written off. Brown still describes the GTI as being 'the most complete car'. There may now be other cars that are quicker and more comfortable to drive, but none has the GTI's 'total package'. Brown talks of 'Malibuising the Rabbit'.

The 'superbunny' sold well in those early years, finding favour with all the leading magazines. As

The GTI 16V has been a consistent winner in the US Showroom Stock class and in the Escort series.

John Rettie recalls: 'every time you saw somebody driving one, they had a big smile on their face'. Rettie bought a Rabbit GTI himself, selling the Golf to an enthusiast in Newport Beach for the same price he had paid for it in Luxembourg. The cost of federalising it had been a mere $3,000 and much of that had been for the actual test. The car was subsequently to be stolen, but retrieved with a stripped interior. It was not the first time it had attracted a thief; twice the GTI badge had been taken.

The 1983 model year 1.8-litre GTI was good for 90bhp. A Bosch KE-Jetronic fuel-injection system, hydraulic valve lifters and larger intake valves saw this improve to 100hp in 1985, with the introduction of the new shape and the loss of the Rabbit name. That year, *Motor Trend* named the GTI its Car of the Year, an award considered one of the most prestigious in the country. The magazine stated that the GTI headed the field in quality control, comfort and convenience, ride and drive, chassis dynamics, handling and fuel economy.

Reeves Callaway, a man now best known for performing magic with the Chevrolet Corvette, tacked on a turbocharger and intercooler and produced a 150hp conversion capable of 122mph and of accelerating to 60mph in 7.2 seconds.

For 1986 the standard GTI's power went up to 102hp, thanks mainly to Digifant electronic engine management.

In 1987 a 'sporty trim' 102hp model, known as the Golf GT, was added to the range, the 8-valve GTI being dropped and replaced by the 123hp GTI 16V. This was reversed at the beginning of 1990 and, for a while, only the 8-valve was sold. A full 2-litre version of the 16V was known to be on its way, something that was only otherwise available in South Africa. It was, said observers, 'overdue'.

According to one story, it was thought that with a decision to reduce prices across the range, it would be easier just to offer the cheaper 8V. Another says that VW had planned to sell the 2-litre 16V alongside the 8V with the 1990 model year, but was held up by an engine supply problem caused mainly by strikes at its Mexican operation. With the demise of Volkswagen of America's own plant in Westmoreland in 1988, GTI's had been sourced from Germany. The new car and engine

were to be built in VW de Mexico's factory in Puebla.

Certainly, the greater popularity of the Jetta in the United States meant that it had to have the 2-litre engine first for its 1990 GLI specification. Thus, the first 2-litre GTI was not seen until mid-way through 1990, when it was introduced as a 1991 model.

An initial observation about the 2-litre car might be, nice engine, shame about the seat-belts! The difference between the European and the North American GTI 16V was accentuated not only by the engine but also by what is a most frustrating restraint system.

During 1990 only 812 2-litre 16Vs were sold, out of a total of 3,668 GTI's. Volkswagen's competition manager in Britain, Nigel Walker, looked at the possibility of homologating the car for Group N racing in the UK — but nowhere near enough were being bought.

The overall 1990 GTI total was sadly low — a far cry from the mid-1980s when over 20,000 GTI's could be sold in a year. Still, it was an improvement on the 1989 figure of 3,316.

1983 remains the highspot. The previous, incomplete year, 5,983 GTI's were sold in the States. In 1984, the figure fell to 22,867, and then during the year of the change from Mk1 to Mk2, to 19,535. Initially the Mk2 was popular, with sales of 20,194 in 1986. Then the totals dropped rapidly: 10,255 in 1987, 4,392 in 1988, and below the 3,000 mark since.

The idea of a hatchback — seen as a cheap car — has never been as appealing in America as in Europe. To that one can add the fact that, particularly with the influx of sleek Japanese 'me-too' coupés, the bodywork looks more dated on the freeways of the United States than it does elsewhere.

Whereas European competition tends to be seen as other GTI-style hatchbacks, in America potential GTI owners are tempted by a whole range of alternatives, from the Ford Probe GT to the Mazda MX-5 Miata, the Honda CRX Si to the Mitsubishi Eclipse.

The average American GTI owner is well documented. He (80 percent are male) is 29 years old, earns about $46,300 and is usually single. 28

GTI 16V American racing champions:
Alastair Oag (top left),
Peter Schwartzott (bottom left),
Al Salerno (top right),
Jim Brandt (bottom right).

Rally driver Guy Light flew the GTI 16V for Volkswagen in America.

percent are married, 87 percent went to college, and 66 percent can be described as 'upper white collar'.

Volkswagen hoped that in 1991 a decision to reduce prices and to move away from a rebate programme would assist sales of GTI's and other models. A further weapon in its armoury was the *Fahrvergnügen* campaign, a US type of *Vorsprung Durch Technik* which extols the joys of driving. Even Johnny Carson, on his famous chat show, took up the slogan.

The GTI has always been a joy to drive. The fitting of the largest engine found in a production version does not alter that. Indeed, freeway driving shows that the new model combines the old Teutonic familiarity with an appetite for long distances which lends positive pleasure to such journeys. Drive from the San Fernando Valley to San Diego and you arrive fresh and happy in the recognition that acceleration was there at the right time and at the right revs.

Los Angeles Times staff writer, Paul Dean, referred to the car as having 'instant soul'.

Through boring and stroking, Volkswagen's Mexican-built 16V engine has grown to 1984cc. The engine is basically the same: an aluminium head with four valves per cylinder, cast iron block and with Bosch Motronic electronic injection/ignition replacing the KE-Jetronic fuel injection.

The increase in displacement, along with a slight increase in compression ratio from 10.0:1 to 10.8:1, produces 134hp at 5800rpm. The previous figure was 123hp. Torque production is up from 120lb/ft at 4250rpm to 133 lb/ft at 4400 rpm.

The 2-litre GTI — complete with its three way catalyst and oxygen sensor — reaches a top speed of 125mph and performs the standing start to 60mph in 7.8 seconds. This is marginally better than a 1.8-litre in European specification, but blink and you won't spot the difference. Other figures include 0-50mph in 5.7 seconds and 40-60mph in 6.4 seconds.

Fuel economy has been estimated at 22mpg for city driving and 28mpg on the highway. The 114mph 1.8-litre 8V records figures of 25 and 32mpg in manual form and 23 and 38mpg in automatic. Bear in mind, however, that these are US gallons, only 0.8327 of the UK equivalent.

There is no doubt that the 2-litre engine likes the revs to be kept up, preferring to accelerate with the needle nearer the red of the rev counter. On the freeway, there is no need to drop down to fourth for simple lane change and overtaking manoeuvres. However, the long hill on Highway 101, when you are heading north and the claustrophobia of Los Angeles is behind you, does necessitate the drop from fifth to fourth.

On the rare occasion when you find a country lane, then keep the revs up and there is all the exhilaration of driving a European 16V. There may have been a time when Volkswagen felt that the US car's soggier suspension limited its appeal to the American market only; but not now. This is everything a European could want from his GTI.

The one unfortunate aspect is the afore-mentioned safety belts. Federal passive regulations seem to be against finding a restraint of a practical nature. The GTI has no provision for air bags and Volkswagen had decided against motorised seat belts.

The resultant compromise features two manual straps, one of which is attached to the door pillar and which you almost crawl under to sit down. The door closed, this holds you in place and you set off, secure in the knowledge that what you do automatically anyway has been done for you... automatically.

The problem is that you have probably forgotten to snap in place the lap belt!

Then there is the getting out. It is possible to unclip the shoulder belt from its position on the door. However, to quote again from the *Los Angeles Times*, 'That automatically disengages any human brain accustomed to the one-catch-does-it-all system in other cars'.

A number of other changes have been made to the car. Manual height adjustment has replaced the electric system on the Recaro seats, the Blaupunkt sound system now has six speakers and reinforcement plates have been added behind the door handles to deter unauthorised entry. Cruise control has been deleted. Cross-spoke 6-12J x 15.9inch

The ultimate Pike's Peak Golf. Jochi Kleint's 1987 car had twin KKK-turbocharged GTI 16V engines to take it to the top of the 13,000ft mountain.

*The 1991 Mexican-built eight-valve car — again,
known simply as the Volkswagen GTI.*

alloy wheels are the major visual difference from
the 8V model.

The latter now has the option of a three-speed
automatic transmission for the first time on a GTI.
This features a shift lock which prevents the lever
from being moved from park or neutral to one of
the driving gears unless the brake pedal is depress-
ed. Top speed in this configuration is 111mph with
the 0-60mph time up from 8.9 to 11.7 seconds.

Base price for the 1991 model GTI 16V was
$13,070 (the first Rabbit GTI's came in at about
$8,500). However, add California compliance and
those other necessities of the Sunshine State, air-
conditioning and a manual sunroof, and the American buyer was looking at spending $14,420.

It was said of the old Westmoreland-built GTI's
that they were every bit as good as their European
counterparts. ('It works so well, you'd swear it
came from Wolfsburg,' stated *Car and Driver*.)
Experience of the Central American manufactured
car would indicate that it is on a par with anything
from either Westmoreland *or* Wolfsburg.

1987 — A Memorable Racing Year

Unfortunately for those excited by the 2-litre's
racing potential, VWoA withdrew its support from
motorsport at the end of the 1990 season. Before
that, just as in Europe, the GTI had provided the
marque with numerous successes — especially in
1987, said to be the most successful season in
VW's US motorsports history. Asking VW's US
competition boss, Mike Kaptuch, how his cars had
fared that year was to risk a very long answer.

The GTI won four national championships in
1987: the International Motor Sports Association
(IMSA) Firestone Firehawk Touring Class; the
Sports Car Club of America (SCCA) Escort Endurance Championship, Showroom Stock B Class; the
SCCA PRO Rally Production Class; and the SCCA
National Championship, Showroom Stock C —
this last at the Road Atlanta Run-Offs. By scoring
more points than any other manufacturer in any
class, the GTI 16V was declared the Firehawk 'Car
of the Year'.

Easterner Al Salerno was the top GTI driver in the Firehawk series. Like most of the other GTI champions in 1987, Salerno had been driving VWs for some years in the Volkswagen Cup Series (for Golfs) and in showroom stock racing. The arrival of the GTI 16V gave him a chance for the recognition he deserved. Salerno won three races, all three-hour events, at Riverside, Phoenix and Columbus, on his way to the title which he won by a margin of 148 to 98. In all, GTI 16Vs won six of the year's ten races, including two six-hour events.

Alastair Oag and Peter Schwartzott from New York State took the GTI 16V to victory in the Escort series, driving a car prepared by Phoenix Racing and owned by Pate Brothers of Indiana. The team won at Sears Point and Sebring, finishing second twice and third on a couple of other occasions. Two other GTI 16V wins helped contribute to the Manufacturers' Championship.

In the SCCA Run-Offs, Michael Cheung led another three GTI's home for a clean sweep of the Showroom Stock C Class, in what is sometimes referred to as the 'world series' of club racing. Not surprisingly, a preview of the event in SCCA's own magazine stated, 'I'll bet the house and my grandmother that a Volkswagen GTI will win this year'. Nineteen of the twenty-six entrants were so mounted.

The SCCA's seer was wrong, though, in expecting Thomas Van Camp to win, with Cheung not even in the first three. Reportedly, the race involved more place-swapping among the first three than anyone could remember. As the trio approached the flag, Fred Fiala banged into veteran Cheung's rear bumper, sending him past erstwhile leader, John Clark, and on to the gold medal.

'Is this real? Am I dreaming?' asked Cheung, a Volkswagen salesman for Reeves Import Motor Cars in Tampa, Florida.

Also that year, Mark McGowan won the SCCA's Solo I and Solo II Championships in a GTI.

The following season was another great one for VW in US motorsport, leading Volkswagen of America to call the GTI 16V 'the winningest VW ever'. The IMSA Firehawk Endurance Touring Car Championship and the Firehawk Car of the Year award fell to the GTI for the second year running.

In rallying, Guy Light and co-driver Jim Brandt were the men to beat. Having campaigned a GTI throughout 1985 and 1986, Light found that the move up to sixteen valves was enough to give him the 1987 SCCA PRO Rally Production Class title. Victories were recorded in the Barbary Coast, Ojibwe and Press-On Regardless PRO events. As Volkswagen's advertising said at the time, 'The speed of Light is directly proportional to the car he drives'.

Light also came second in Group N on America's only international rally of the year, the Olympus. On the daunting Pike's Peak Auto Hill Climb he won his class, setting a new record time.

In 1985 Volkswagen had developed a 390hp twin-engined Golf to compete on that renowned mountain. That, too, must warrant mention, for in its initial form it was powered by a couple of Oettinger 1.8-litre GTI engines, one in the rear. This resulted in a 0-60mph time of 4.6 seconds and a top speed of 162mph. 1979 European Rally Champion Jochi Kleint was the intrepid pilot, but by the time the car had reached the top of the mountain it was running out of steam. Kleint was beaten by Michele Mouton's Audi quattro, a more conventional means of four-wheel drive.

The following year, a pair of turbocharged 1.3-litre Polo engines were fitted, but the power band was very narrow and it was back to Golf motivation for the final attempt on the 'Race to the Clouds' in 1987. Built in Austria, the all-new car had a pair of 16-valve, 1.8-litre GTI units fitted with KKK turbochargers and each giving over 300bhp. Both were mounted longitudinally instead of transversely, the reason for turning the engines being to use Hewland gearboxes which would allow a precise choice of ratios for each gear.

Kleint again drove the car, the centre part of which was built in monocoque construction. It may have used GTI engines, but it was a long way from John Rettie's original dream.

8 Buying a Golf GTI

by Robin Wager, Editor

VWmotoring

As we have seen already in this book, Volkswagen's Golf GTI really was the daddy of all the 'hot hatches'. Despite nearly every other manufacturer having followed suit, I believe (and here I should perhaps declare a bias resulting from some 14 years' editorial involvement with the UK's premier Volkswagen magazine) that it retains its position as the best of the bunch.

VW build-quality and durability make the GTI a particularly good bet secondhand, and a little time spent in diligent searching for a cared-for example can reward even the buyer on a relatively small (by today's new-car price standards) budget.

A glance at the relevant publications will quickly show that used GTIs are not exactly difficult to find; there are, however, as always, the good, the bad and the positively ugly!

The basic principles of buying secondhand are similar to those for any used car. Firstly, do you aim to buy from a private seller or a dealer? The answer depends to a certain extent on your ability to spot a 'dog'! If you are not confident about this, the respectable trade outlet is the better bet every time.

Franchised Volkswagen dealers' prices will generally be the highest for a given year and model; but you should gain the advantage of knowledgeable pre-sale preparation, backed up by a good after-sale warranty.

Next comes a category of dealer well worth exploring: the GTI specialist. Several of these have sprung up in recent years, dealing more or less exclusively in 'hot hatches' — although not always exclusively in VWs.

Finally there is the private seller — usually offering the lowest price, but with no warranties or comebacks afterwards. The choice is yours, but I have heard so many sad stories of cash being handed over to complete strangers ('He seemed such a nice guy') for mobile rust-heaps with shiny paintwork, that I can only emphasise the one bit of Latin that every used car buyer should know: *caveat emptor*.

Having decided on your budget, the next question is what model and age of GTI to go for. Since we expect this book to be around indefinitely, it would be pointless to quote actual price examples; at the risk of stating the obvious, older cars are generally cheaper — but with one or two quirks to that generalisation.

As the Golf gets older (particularly with the launch of the Mk3), *aficionados* have come to regard the Mk1 as something of a classic. In fact, the 'Campaign' model — the late Mk1 with 1.8-litre engine and special equipment — is recognised as a classic already, thanks to its limited numbers.

Good examples of the Giugiaro-designed Mk1, more distinctive-looking than the in-house styled successor, are now sought after by the true VW enthusiast and the young, impecunious poseur alike, their inherent durability and performance combining to make them a worthwhile buy.

As with most VWs, there are a goodly number of left-hand-drive versions around in Britain. Launched at the Frankfurt Show in 1975, the GTI was introduced into the UK about a year later in left-hand-drive form only; it was not until July 1979 that RHD models became available, at which time the car's success with UK buyers was assured.

While left-hookers will be cheaper to buy, beware the inevitable insurance loading: unless you do much Continental travelling, my advice would be to pay a little more for an RHD example.

As we already know, Mk1 cars had a 110bhp, 1.6-litre engine with Bosch K-Jetronic fuel injection. This was used until September 1982, when the new 1.8-litre (but with just two more bhp) was installed. The combination of Mk1 body and larger engine lasted for only about 18 months, the Mk2 Golf being launched here in May 1984.

Many buyers will be tempted by the drophead version, the VAG (UK) naming of which fluctuated between Convertible and Cabriolet, almost according to whether or not there was 'R' in the month!

Whilst it can be wholeheartedly recommended as a sound buy, it is as well to be aware of the pitfalls of the convertible model. Firstly, insurance again: the premiums (especially if you can't garage it) are likely to be high. And, if you can't garage it, the hood will suffer premature ageing and/or vandalism, and that is an expensive item to renew.

The Convertible's luggage-space is almost non-existent, a point to take into account *before* you embark on a tour of Europe with four occupants!

It's surprising how often I have asked non-VW buffs if they can spot a major difference between the Mk2 Golf hatchback and the Convertible (apart from the hood, that is), and found that they can't. There is one, of course — the Convertible has always been based on the *Mk1* body style, since the production volume did not justify tooling up for the Mk2. There will, however, be a ragtop version of

Golf 3 — built, like its predecessors, under contract by Karmann of Osnabrück.

Given the desirability of the Convertible and the classic status of the Mk1-bodied cars, there is little doubt that the current Convertibles are destined to become collectors' cars in the years to come.

Note that not all Convertibles are GTIs: there was always at least one carburettor-engined model listed and a GTI, by definition, has fuel injection!

So, having absorbed this background information to decide more or less on your target car, what points should you look for in order to avoid the equivalent of stuffing your hard-earned readies down the nearest drain?

The good news is that GTIs wear and age well — so well, in fact, that it is fairly difficult to pinpoint specific GTI problem areas. As I have said, the basics apply regardless of make, so firstly have a good look all round and along the car. You're looking for signs of ripply bodywork, or oversprayed paint on rubbers, trim or lights.

If you find any, at best the car has had some cosmetic attention to stone-chips or scratches; at worst, it might be the halves of two separate cars welded together! The body panels are prone to car park dings but, if the owner has been diligent with the touch-up paint, rust should not be a problem. Only very early cars can be expected to show actual corrosion in door panels etc.

Look at the general condition, especially the interior, to see if it corresponds to age and mileage (how worn are the pedal rubbers?). The interior trim, incidentally, wears well, which helps to contribute to secondhand value.

If all seems well, ask to see the car's service book. A main dealer or specialist service history bodes well, provided the stamps are at about the right mileages and the oil change intervals, in particular, have not been severely prolonged — the best way I know to shorten engine life. A 'lost' service record should be regarded with great suspicion, and never accept a promise to 'forward it when it turns up'.

Although it doesn't in any way guarantee the car's condition, the MoT certificate is important: a test recently carried out should at least mean no immediate heavy expenditure to make the car roadworthy.

Auctions are an option for the used car buyer, though not always advisable for the inexperienced. Here, a VAG lease/contract rental fleet GTI comes under the hammer at ADT Auctions' premises in Blackbushe, Surrey.

Ask to drive the car, preferably from cold, and check the gearchange. Syncromesh can become tired, particularly if the car has been thrashed, and especially on second gear (worse when cold). On a higher-mileage car, note the overall quality of the change, since this can become generally sloppy as a result of wear in the shift mechanism at the base of the lever — not desperately expensive to remedy in terms of parts, but labour-intensive.

Listen to the engine (albeit a tough unit) for the usual threatening noises like slack bearings. Once warmed up, check in the mirror for exhaust smoke, especially after descending a long hill on the over-run — a sure sign of worn valve guides and hence not a little expense. Check that the exhaust is not blowing.

Worn driveshafts can be expensive, too, so manoeuvre the car on full lock with the windows open and listen for any tell-tale knocks. It's worth getting down on your hands and knees to inspect the rubber boots on the CV joints: if they're split and the grease has oozed out, then damage has probably already occurred.

While you're down there, check the condition of the tyres, whether they show any irregular wear (possibly steering geometry or even chassis mis-alignment) and whether they're a matching set.

The GTI is renowned for its taut handling, so any tendency to pitching, bouncing, wallowing or pulling to one side should be regarded with suspicion. The most likely cause is worn out shock absorbers.

With an early car, check all the electrical equipment, since we've seen more than our share of problems in this department at *VW Motoring*. They can usually be traced to a faulty fuse/relay board, renewal of which often proves the only solution.

Robin Wager is editor of *VW Motoring*, the mainstream UK magazine for Volkswagen and Audi owners. A chartered accountant, he found himself increasingly intrigued by the debits and credits of cars, finally forsaking the profession in 1973 to become assistant editor of *Safer Motoring*, as the magazine was then known. A 4,000 miles-in- a-fortnight tour of Scandinavia, co-driving a friend's car, had already hooked him on Beetles, and he has since owned a succession of them (starting with a fifties split-window model), as well as later VWs and Audis. Since taking over as editor in 1982, Robin has 'rationalised' the magazine's title and successfully presided over the ongoing changes necessary to keep *VW Motoring* at the forefront of the Volkswagen scene, embracing as it does everything from the original air-cooled cars to the latest high-tech V.A.G. range. The constant feedback received through the magazine, from readers and trade alike, puts him in a unique position to compile this chapter.

If you can, at some stage drive behind your prospective purchase, or watch it being driven on the road, and check that it isn't 'crabbing' sideways. If it is, say goodbye to the vendor NOW!

Brakes have always been a source of contention with Golfs, and the GTI in particular. The RHD conversion features a cross-linkage which creates free play, giving long pedal travel and brakes which can feel 'dead'. Be assured that this is normal, and more so on earlier cars! There are some specialist tweaks and conversions which can help, but more important to the buyer is to check the conditions of the brakes themselves.

The sliding calipers are prone to seizure if not regularly dismantled and freed of dirt (something dealers are strangely reluctant to do, since it is not in the service schedule); this in turn leads to one pad bearing on one side of the disc and wearing it unevenly. The remedy will almost certainly be new discs and pads, and, in severe cases, new calipers too — again not cheap, although GTIs do tend to get through brake discs and so wear in these alone should not be regarded as too important.

The engine should be free of oil and fluid leaks, although its general appearance may leave something to be desired due to corrosion of the alloy and exposed parts. This is normal and can be much improved with some WD40 spray and the re-application of VAG's engine bay wax to the sheet metal — a factory recommendation, especi- ally if the compartment has been steam-cleaned.

Whilst looking under the bonnet, check the bulk-head where the clutch cable passes through its large rubber grommet. Cracking of metal around this point, through fatigue, is common and results in loss of clutch action, while repair involves welding in a reinforcing plate.

Moving to the other end, open the hatch and

check inside the boot. There will almost inevitably be scratches from luggage on the suspension turrets, but a more important check is to lift the boot matting and check that the floor is dry. Any signs of dampness or mould would suggest a water leak — not only potentially difficult to cure, but possibly indicative of a rear-end shunt at some time.

Regarding the Convertible in particular: be certain firstly that you really do want open-air motoring, and not just the 'pose value'. And, unless your budget is really tight, don't be tempted into buying the first high-mileage ragtop you see: there are plenty around with low mileage which have been used as second cars.

The condition of the hood is important, of course, as the rest of the car won't last long if it's faulty. Leaks will be evidenced by stained seats and carpets, possibly even a damp interior. If the car *smells* at all damp, leave it alone.

It's especially important to test drive a Convertible thoroughly, since the body is rather less taut and the interior fittings and trim tend to rattle and squeak more than in a hatchback. Drive it with the hood down, and make sure you feel comfortable in it.

So, having made your checks, does your prospective purchase have good paint, sound bodywork, engine free of smoke and odd noises, clean, fresh interior, normal handling? Does it *feel* right? Then go ahead and deal, and congratulations — you've bought a great little car!

9 Care and Maintenance of the Golf GTI

Note: This complete servicing guide to the Golf GTI was compiled by the staff of Practical Motorist *magazine, where it was first published.*
We acknowledge with thanks the editor's kind permission to include it in this book.

A front-runner as far as technology goes, the Golf GTI has standard equipment which includes hydraulic tappets, computerised engine management system, self-adjusting cable-clutch and maintenance-free electronic ignition.

If you are thinking that this means the GTI needs no servicing, you would be wrong. Admittedly there is less engine maintenance than you would expect, but there is plenty to do elsewhere.

Volkswagen's major service is carried out every 20,000 miles. In addition, the company recommends a comprehensive inspection every twelve months and an oil change in-between. Assuming an owner covers 10,000 miles a year, the car would need an oil-change every 5,000 miles, supplemented by an inspection every 10,000 miles. The service schedule on this page is based on this annual mileage.

The picture guide which follows looks at the main points of a 20,000-mile service. The GTI illustrated is a Mk2 16-valve version. Apart from the cylinder head, service-wise, the 8-valve GTI 1.8-litre is more or less the same. Any differences are identified in the text. The jobs have been graded for the do-it-yourself mechanic. A star indicates an easy task. One to five cuss-marks (!) indicate the degree of difficulty.

SERVICE SCHEDULE

EVERY 5,000 MILES OR SIX MONTHS
Change engine oil and filter.

EVERY 10,000 MILES OR TWELVE MONTHS
As 5,000 miles plus:
Check lighting systems, signals and horn.
Check/top up battery electrolyte.
Check engine for leaks.
Test strength of anti-freeze.
Check brake fluid level.
Clutch pedal clearance (early models): check and adjust if necessary.
Check wiper action, add screenwash solvent and top up washer reservoir.
Grease door check straps, oil hinges.
Check disc brake pad thickness.
Examine braking system for leaks.
Check steering tie rods and rack gaiters.
Visually check drive shaft CV joints for leaks.
Check steering column joints.
Check tyre pressures, inflate if necessary.
Check tyre tread depth and wear patterns.
Check headlamp settings.
Road test to check action of handbrake, brake pedal, gearshift and steering.
Check idling speed and CO, adjust if necessary.

EVERY 20,000 MILES
As twelve months plus:
Check drive belt condition and tension.
Renew spark plugs.
Renew air cleaner element.
Renew brake hydraulic fluid.
Clean and lubricate sliding roof guide rails.
Visually check underbody sealant.

L U B R I C A T I O N

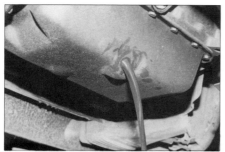

1. DRAIN ENGINE OIL ★

(Left) Easy. The drain plug is in the centre of the rear of the sump, so all the oil will dribble out if you drive the car up on the ramps. VW recommends its own synthetic oil. With a filter change you need 4 litres for a 16V or 4.5 litres for an 8V GTI. Fit a new copper washer when you replace the plug.

2.CHANGE OIL FILTER !

(Left, below) Tucked up between the front of the block and the grille, it is not easy to reach. It might be best to use a large pair of grips to loosen it — there is not much room to swing a strap-wrench.

I G N I T I O N

3. RENEW SPARK PLUGS (1) ★

(Right) The 16-valve engine has its four plugs buried deep under the camshaft cover — this is a plug cap and VW thoughtfully provides a handle on the top to enable you to lift them out.

4. RENEW SPARK PLUGS (2) ★

(Right, below) The recommended plugs have three electrodes and a small (16mm) hexagon. They are expensive but should last 20,000 miles. You will need a socket with a rubber insert fixed to a long extension to get the old plugs out and the new ones in. On the 8-valve engine, the plugs are on the side of the head facing the radiator and are much easier to reach. Plugs should tighten to 21 lb/ft.

5. CHECK HT ★

(Below) There are no contact breaker points, so the only reason for taking off the distributor cap is if you suspect the ignition is tracking. Make sure the inside of the cap is clean and, when refitted, pull out the 'king lead' from the coil and check it is making a sound connection. If the end of the cable is burnt, fit a new one.

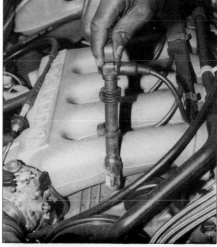

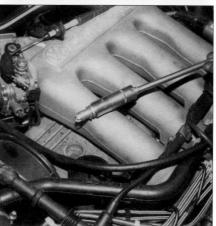

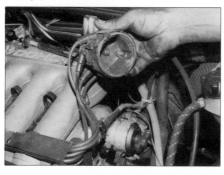

FUEL SYSTEM

6. RENEW AIR FILTER ★

(Top, right) The filter is hidden away under the metering unit for the fuel injection. Pull away a small plastic cover behind the radiator grille, then undo four over-centre clips to release the cover. The large paper element filter will come away with the cover. Fit the new one in the box underneath and clip down the cover.

7. FUEL FILTER ★

(Right, second from top) Under the car on the offside, just ahead of the rear axle, you will find the high pressure pump for the fuel injection system. Alongside it is this large canister, which is the fuel filter. In theory it should last the life of the car, but if the fuel injection goes wrong, this filter is the first component to change.

8. ADJUST IDLING SPEED ★

(Right, third from top) Idling speed is 1,000rpm plus or minus 50rpm and is adjusted by moving this air screw. Usually only a fraction of a turn is needed.

9. CHECK CO LEVEL !

(Right, bottom) VW dealers use this complex machine to check the amount of carbon monoxide in the exhaust gas, which should be 1% plus or minus 0.5%. The machine also provides a full engine check.

10. ADJUSTING CO LEVEL ★

(Below) If you have a CO meter and know how to use it, this is where you find the small Allen screw which adjusts the mixture. The setting is carried out with the crankcase ventilation pipe to the air cleaner disconnected, and the cable from the idle stabiliser disconnected (the stabiliser is a small canister on the nearside end of the cylinder head which is connected by a pipe to the inlet trunking).

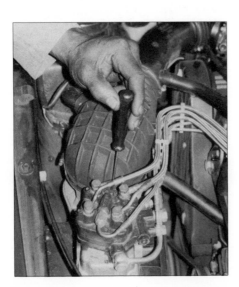

TRANSMISSION

11. CHECK DRIVE SHAFT GAITERS ★
(Top, left) There are two on each drive shaft. With the front wheels hanging down, check them visually while rotating each wheel.

12. FINAL DRIVE OIL LEAKS ★
(Top, right) Oil has been known to leak from behind the inner drive shaft couplings — check the oil seal is dry at the point where the drive shaft leaves the differential coupling.

13. CLUTCH ADJUSTMENT ★
(Left) The clutch cable sprouts vertically from the gearbox on the nearside. In fact, this cable is self-adjusting. Earlier models have a manually-adjusted cable with a threaded plastic end-piece. Adjust it so there is around 1/4in clearance between the outer cable and its abutment on the gearbox when the outer cable is fitted.

BRAKES

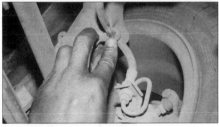

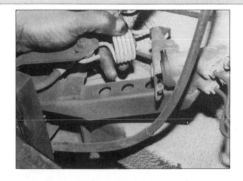

14. CHECK BRAKE HOSES ★
(Above) All flexible hoses are easy to check with the car raised — renew them at the first sign of chafing, perishing or leakage.

15. COMPENSATOR ★
(Top, right) A compensator valve, which reduces pressure to the rear calipers when the brakes are applied hard, is mounted underneath, near the rear axle. Check the unions are not leaking and the rocker arm connected to the spring moves freely.

16. FRONT PADS ★
(Right) The experts can tell the thickness of the outer disc pad by peering at it through the wheel aperture. However, it is best to take the wheel off in order to get a good view of both pads through this aperture in the caliper. Renew the pads if the combined thickness of the pad and the backing plate is reduced to 7mm.

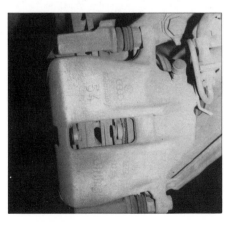

17. REAR PADS ★

(Top, right) The same rules on pad wear apply at the rear. If rear or front pads need changing, loosen the upper caliper mounting bolt and remove the bottom one. The caliper can then be swung up, leaving the pads behind. Retract the piston before swinging the caliper down over the new pads.

18. HANDBRAKE ★

(Right) One handbrake cable each side is connected to this lever which operates the rear pads. Check the lever is free to move and make sure the rear wheel rotates smoothly with the handbrake off. The handbrake should only use up two clicks of the ratchet before the rear brakes come on. If it needs adjustment, prise up the small lid at the rear of the handbrake cover and take out the screw underneath. Lift off the cover and there will be one or two adjusting nuts

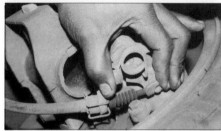

S T E E R I N G

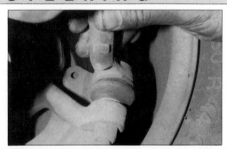

19. TRACK-RODS & RACK GAITERS ★

(Left) The track-rod ends are easy enough to find. Make sure the rubber seals are undamaged. The steering rack is tucked out of the way above the lower suspension arms. Check the gaiters are not leaking.

L E V E L S

20. BRAKE FLUID !!

(Right) The hydraulic reservoir is on the offside sandwiched between the air intake trunking and the suspension turret. It is difficult to find, the level is not easy to read and topping up is difficult too.

21. COOLANT ★

(Bottom, right) Standard procedure every 10,000 miles is to check the anti-freeze content with a hydrometer. The level is marked on the outside of the translucent plastic header tank.

22. WASHER ★

(Below) Current GTI models have a huge 4.2-litre washer bottle serving front and rear screens. Empty, it takes a full bottle of Quantum Screenwash Additive. If it is half full, use half a bottle and top up with water.

G E N E R A L

23. DRIVE BELT ★
(Left) It is a bit of a squeeze on the offside, but at least the alternator is accessible if the tension needs adjusting. Check the condition of the rubbing surfaces of the belt for cracks and damage. The belt should deflect about 1/2in between the two top pulleys under firm thumb pressure.

24. EXHAUST SYSTEM ★
(Left, second from top) This GTI had four silencers. All should be checked for leaks. At the same time, make sure the hangers are holding it firmly and are not split or perished.

25. SUNROOF ★
(Left, third from top) Standard equipment on the Mk2 16V, the steel sunroof should be lubricated with something like WD40. Use it on the cable guides on each side and the springs behind the front deflector. Take care not to squirt oil inside the car.

26. TYRES ★
(Left, fourth from top) When checking tyre pressures, do not forget the 'space saver' in the floor of the boot. It should be inflated to 60psi.

27. DOORS & HINGES ★
(Bottom, left) Creaky doors suggest that someone has not been greasing the check-straps. Grease the upper and lower surfaces and use an oil-can to apply a few drops of engine oil to the hinges.

V E R D I C T !

For a high-performance car, the Golf GTI is remarkably easy to look after. Much of the credit goes to the engine management system which automatically takes care of such things as ignition timing and fuel metering, while hydraulic tappets (1986 on) mean that no valve adjustment is needed.

Practical Motorist's gripes are few. The brake fluid reservoir is not easy to check or top up — presumably a result of a left-hand-drive design being modified for right-hand-drive. And unless you have a CO meter, tinkering with the fuel system is inadvisable except for adjusting the idling speed. On the 16-valve the oil filter is awkwardly placed at the nearside of the cam cover, so you must use a funnel when topping up.

The synthetic oil and the spark plugs VW recommends are expensive, but this should be no problem if you have been able to buy and insure a GTI. *Practical Motorist* would not recommend using cheap alternatives.

For ease of servicing, *Practical Motorist* awards the Golf GTI just one cuss-mark.

John Stevens. Course Manager for the
Golf GTI School and Chief Instructor of the
Audi Quattro High Performance School, John
Stevens has been described as the 'guru' of
high performance driving.

He has worked as a consultant on performance driving with the police and has been
invited to lecture at police driving schools.
In 1989 and 1990 he worked in South Africa to
set up a High Performance School at Kyalami
Grand Prix Circuit and to produce
instructional and pro- motional videos. He
coaches drivers at all levels of motorsport,
including Grand Prix.

Employed by sponsors such as Shell and
Marlboro, he specialises in accompanying
teams to circuits throughout the world to teach
their drivers the ultimate lines.

He also coaches in rallying and motorcycle
racing.

*We'll show you how! A gathering of GTI instructors on
one of the early courses.*

10 Driving the Golf GTI: Making the Most of Your Hot Hatch

September 1989 saw the start of GTI Driving Courses, organised by Volkswagen's UK importer. Intended for GTI owners and potential owners, the course uses private circuits — Silverstone, Goodwood, Castle Combe and Oulton Park — Golf and Jetta GTI models and a team of fully qualified advanced driving tutors who were led, initially, by racer Andrew Gilbert-Scott. Throughout the day-long session, students are accompanied by the same instructor in groups of three. The total number of participants per day is 12.

During 1991 the philosophy of the course altered slightly. Changes at Milton Keynes brought it into the same department as the equivalent Audi course and under the control of John Stevens, one of the country's leading high performance driving instructors, who coaches even the Formula One stars. Stevens removed the slalom and avoidance tuition that had been part of the early courses, feeling that within the time available it was better to concentrate on achieving a high level of proficiency in one discipline, rather than to attempt three or four. The standard demanded from the instructors is very high indeed; only occasionally is one selected from the continuous stream of applicants. Team member, Tim Jones, has described the Audi and Golf GTI courses as the 'jewels in the crown' for high performance driving instructors.

All the concentration is on driving technique, and with good reason, as will be explained. The courses are not cheap, but in the short time they have been running they have been highly praised in the press. As *The Times* pointed out, they are not full of 'eager yuppies keen to drive ridiculously fast, but men and women, with an average age around 35'. You really do find solicitors and accountants on these events.

The courses prove that learning can also be entertaining, which could account for the fact that pupils are known come back for more. Stephen Westray, sales executive at Preston Volkswagen dealership, Fairways, is one such. Having experienced both the old- and new-style GTI courses, he has found them both beneficial and (one only has to see the grin on his face during the day) fun.

'You got up to higher speeds the second time, there being no cones to navigate in the morning,' Westray observed, 'and I probably learnt more, having already been on one course.' Instructors, despite all being highly skilled, naturally vary, and it may also have been that the second instructor was more painstaking and less inclined to let pupils have their head.

'Both days were brilliant,' Westray concluded.

The whole focus of the course is on improving clients' road driving in terms of competence and

The author adjusts his driving-mirror before driving out on the Oulton Park circuit. GTI Driving Course instructor Tim Jones watches carefully. Jones, a former racer and son of Brands Hatch commentator Brian Jones, has been an instructor on various courses since leaving the Royal Navy. Himself a pupil of John Stevens, Jones is now one of the hand-picked team for which competition is fierce and only the best are chosen.

safety. The accent is not on driving fast, but on driving well. Road driving itself can be divided into two categories: road craft and technique. Road craft is how we conduct ourselves on the road. Technique is the way in which we drive the car, and it is the latter discipline that is the basis of the course.

It must be said that the performance of the modern saloon car has changed out of all recognition in the last 20 years. Apart from the innumerable high performance models on the market, even the humble 1.6-litre family saloon can now achieve 100mph, with acceleration, braking and cornering ability to match. Correct technique must therefore be a vital aspect of modern driving.

The courses are held at racing circuits for specific reasons. It eliminates the problems and frustrations of oncoming traffic and, since all vehicles are travelling in the same direction, it allows pupils to experiment and make mistakes in complete safety. It enables pupils to concentrate exclusively on their driving and provides a repetitive situation whereby, if they make a mistake on a corner, they will be driving through it again in, say, two minutes' time and so can practise until they get it right.

The course begins with a lecture from John Stevens on driving technique. 'We are concentrating today on the relationship between driving technique and car handling and performance; or, in simple terms, how the way you drive will affect the handling of your car.' Stevens explains how traditionally taught methods of driving technique have little relationship to modern car design and performance. 'Some 50 years ago, a group of considered experts worked out a perfectly logical system of actions that a driver should take when he drives a car. What they failed to consider was the effect those actions would have on the car itself!' Vehicle dynamics are discussed, together with the forces acting on a car in a given situation. These concern constant elements such as centrifugal force, and variable elements that can be generated by the driver.

'In a highly technical sport like golf, a performer can have variations in grip and swing and still be a world-class player, simply because the human body is itself variable and adaptable. When a designer creates a car, however, he is working strictly within the laws of physics, dynamics and mechanics. These laws and their effects are immutable, so there is only one sequence of actions when driving a car in a particular road situation that can allow the vehicle to operate not only at 100 percent efficiency but, more importantly, at the maximum margin of safety. Any variation of these actions will produce an adverse variation in the result.'

Attention is given to the seating position. When you adjust your seat, your left knee should still be bent when you depress the clutch pedal to the floor. In an accident situation, where the driver would naturally brace himself with his feet, if the left leg is straight the impact is generated up the leg, through the hip and up the spine. If the knee is bent only slightly, then flexing of the leg takes place and the shock is absorbed by the seat belts.

Seat adjustment is also related to how you hold the steering-wheel. 'You should be able to hold the top of the wheel comfortably, with your elbows slightly bent, in order to keep your hands in their original position as far as possible when steering the car. This will mean crossing your hands when necessary. The present method of shuffling the wheel is an excellent initial method for teaching a learner-driver to steer, or for turning left or right at road junctions. When driving on the open road, however, one can only have maximum control over the car if one's hands are in their original position. In this way, the driver establishes a reference between the position of the steering-wheel and the front wheels of the car. He instinctively knows how much correction to give to the steering in any emergency situation. Any action requiring precision and dexterity must, in an emergency, be instinctive so that the driver can react with sufficient speed.

'Many drivers demonstrate that, on a skid pan, they can control the car by shuffling the wheel while steering. It must be remembered, however, that the surface grip on a skid pan resembles ice. The car is travelling at only 15 to 20mph, and the driver makes the car skid before he controls it. In other words, it is predictable and it happens quite slowly. On the public road, a skid will probably happen at between 50 and 70mph. It will be very violent and completely *un*predictable. When cor-

Tim Jones talks the author out of the hairpin at Oulton Park.

rection is applied, if the road is merely wet, the car will flick back to a straight line or over-correct the other way very quickly. Shuffling the wheel will give neither the necessary speed nor the required precision of correction.'

Stevens continues the briefing by discussing cornering, which he divides into three main sections: the approach, which covers braking and gear-changing; cornering bends; and, finally, the dynamics of car behaviour.

'When braking hard, about 70 percent of the weight of the car goes over the front. The nose goes down and becomes heavy, the back rises and becomes light, and if one tried to change direction in that situation, the car would be unstable. It is sensible therefore to complete one's braking and gear-changing before one turns into a corner, in order to allow the car to settle back into its normal operating plane.

'In so many training programmes, much emphasis is placed on smooth, rather than efficient, driving. People frequently relate smoothness to doing everything slowly. This can mean that directly they try to make progress, they tend to do everything too late. The aim is to be an efficient driver. One can be a smooth driver and not much good at anything else, but if one is efficient one will automatically be smooth.

'Braking should not be heavy, but positive, with the gear-change completed at about two-thirds of the braking distance. Braking and changing gear together allows for a higher degree of precision when reducing speed, and therefore a wider margin of safety.'

Stevens explains that the training relating to cornering lines is a purely technical exercise, and that the best line through a corner is not always possible on the road.

'When approaching a corner on a public road, you must always be able to stop within the distance you can see. If a corner has high banks or trees on either side, and limited visibility, it may be necessary to go in much deeper in order to be able to look further ahead. When you acquire the ability to assess the technically correct line through a corner, you are safer on the wrong lines because you are able to think ahead of the action and know how it will affect the handling of the car. On a

race-track you never look at a corner, because if you do, you will always look to the outside and that is where you will drive to. You always look round corners, just as you should on the road. Every time you leave one corner, you are planning where to position the car for the next one. Again, exactly as you should on a public road.'

Strong emphasis is placed on braking, as it is considered a weak point with the majority of drivers.

'So many drivers change gear first and brake afterwards. It gets to the stage where if you shout "brake", they react by changing gear. You can imagine how dangerous this would be in an emergency situation on the road!

'Another common fault is that when drivers do brake, they do not do it positively. They will transfer their foot to the brake-pedal and for 30 yards or so will do nothing else; then they will brake far too hard at the last moment.'

All the training on cornering lines is related to car behaviour.

'When cornering, you can take a line of constant radius or a line of variable radius. If you wish to travel through a corner without accelerating, the line of constant radius is ideal. However, if you wish to accelerate hard out of the corner, particularly if you have a turbocharged car where the power can come in suddenly, you need a line of variable radius. This entails going into the corner slightly deeper and making a slightly tighter turn. You will then have a much flatter curve exiting the corner where a sudden increase in propulsion will not affect the stability of the car.

'The primary aim of the Golf GTI School is to develop a sound knowledge of driving technique commensurate with the sophistication of modern car technology and design. A frequent quote from pupils is, "When I came here today, I thought I could drive. Now I realise I can't, but if I practise what I have learned, I might *become* a good driver". If pupils go away with that motivation, with all the discipline, precision and concentration it entails, then I feel the course must be a significant contribution to road safety.'

11 Show Time:
Celebrating the Golf GTI

A cold, wet and windy August Bank Holiday 1986 saw the largest-ever gathering of Golf GTIs in the UK, a total said to equal in number that at the previous year's European convention, the Treffen. The occasion, a race meeting at Silverstone, was to mark the tenth anniversary of the GTI.

Volkswagen sponsored the day's proceedings which commenced with a race for the smaller cars in the British Saloon Car Championship. Alan Minshaw's Mk2 took the lead during the very last lap to prove whose day it was.

Once Alan Padden had thrown his VW-sponsored Pitts Special around the skies, over 100 GTIs from far and wide, including the Continent, came out for a parade of the Northamptonshire circuit. GTi Engineering's turbocharged Mk2 led the way. An original plan to drive one lap to Wood-cote Corner was shelved as everyone drove round twice, the entire track being filled by GTIs. Elsewhere in the car park a further 900 machines were assembled — nearly four percent of all the GTI and GTI convertibles sold in the UK by that date.

The zenith of the GTI fraternity's year, though, is the International GTI Treffen (or meeting), the first of which took place in 1982. Within two years it had merited an entry in the *Guinness Book of Records*, a year later attracting over 3,000 GTI folk.

The good and the great were seen at the event, with 1975, 1977 and 1984 Formula One World Champion Niki Lauda opening the fifth Treffen,

and Dr Carl Hahn, Chairman of Volkswagen AG, performing the honours the following year.

That particular event, the 1987 festival, saw the first organised trip by British GTI owners. In cars festooned in Union Jacks and with drivers clad in specially printed T-shirts, the British drove down to the Austrian lakeside village, Maria Wörth. According to Club GTI secretary David Pipes, a standard GTI was hard to find. 'Modifications ranged from the subtle to the outrageous,' he recalls.

Specialist tuning firms lined up, with such as Koni, Pirelli and Kamei in the trade exhibition. A four-wheel-drive four-door GTI 16V was available for a mere £24,999. However, Pipes was quick to notice that the produce on show was generally much cheaper than in Britain.

Activities ranged from driving tests at nearby Klagenfurt to bonfires and fireworks. High point of the festival was a 25-ton (yes, ton!) GTI made from granite which was pulled 600 metres on a sledge to a final resting-place by the lakeside gardens.

In 1988 visitors were estimated at around 2,000. That Volkswagen was now looking ahead of the GTI was illustrated by the first public showing of the G60 supercharged, four-wheel-drive Rallye Golf. Initially, VW's engineers were reluctant even to open the bonnet. What was being shown was not necessarily the production version, as the company was using the Treffen to discover what typical GTI owners thought before deciding upon the final specification. Other design studies at the gathering

*Subtle body styling leads the parade around
Silverstone's Woodcote corner on the GTI's 10th
anniversary.*

indicated that, for the remainder of its production
life, VW wanted to move the GTI, especially the
16V, upmarket with a series of luxury limited
editions.

A GTI even flew that year. Slung beneath a
parachute and towed by a motorboat, a red BBS-
sponsored version made a couple of circuits of the
lake before landing on the water. On the final day
of that year's Treffen, a few hundred GTIs set off
on a pre-planned route taking them into Yugoslavia and to Bled where an alternative Treffen had
reportedly attracted less than 20 cars!

Club GTI was celebrating its first birthday at the
event and was the centre of much attention, including an interview for West German television.

Unlike previous events, the 1989 Treffen was
held without any visible assistance from Volkswagen, something which led to some of the tuning
and accessory suppliers not bothering to par-
ticipate. Organisation was in the hands of the
DCGE, the international federation of GTI clubs.
The police were out in force, even imposing an

on-the-spot-fine for wheel-spinning, irrespective
of speed. Those who wanted to compete had both
sprint and slalom laid on at the fabled Österreichring.

David Pipes noticed a definite trend in the modifications that had been carried out. Few of the Mk2
cars featured Zender-style kits, owners preferring
engine, suspension and wheel and tyre changes
rather than bodykits. Where the latter had been
fitted, they tended to be ultra-wide and from such
as Rieger, the Rallye Sport Shop, the Special Car
Center and Kerscher. The fact that price-lists included 11x5-inch wheels indicated just how wide
some of the bodykits were.

In May 1990, more so than in 1989, many of the
events were staged some way from the central
point of Reifnitz. Again the Österreichring at Zelt-
weg was on the agenda. This time the idea was to
drive almost a full lap of the old six-kilometre
Austrian Grand Prix circuit at an average speed of
70km/h. The winner is said to have recorded
69.9999!

Over 1,000 GTIs, worth an estimated eight million pounds, were to be found at the Treffen in 1984.

Perhaps more than anything else the International Treffen illustrates the cameraderie of the Golf GTI fraternity. However, it is necessary to register with the organisers, as only a certain number of cars can be accepted owing to an agreement with the local authorities. Nevertheless, around 1,400 GTIs may be resident for the five-day duration, together with several hundred day visitors.

For those unable to travel to the Continent, the 1988 GTI International at Knebworth, Hertfordshire, in September provided a suitable alternative. Over 150 GTIs were seen in the car-park on the first day, but only 25 were entered for the concours, won by Roy Craig's black Mk1. The following day saw over 200 cars visiting the event. It should be pointed out, however, that the weather was appalling and that a postal strike had prevented much of the pre-event publicity arriving on time.

The following year saw the event move to the Transport and Road Research Laboratory at Crowthorne, Berkshire. The date moved forward to early

May and the weather was greatly improved. The change of location meant that drivers' competitions, such as a sprint and a slalom, could be organised. Over 100 entrants took part in the former. National Autotest champion John North was, perhaps not surprisingly, the winner of the latter.

The third and fourth GTI Internationals were also held at the TRRL, again attracting visitors from Germany. Most popular event in 1990 was reportedly the standing-start quarter-mile sprint organised by Club GTI, two cars running side by side. For the first time, even a fashion show was on the agenda, Rohan Designs showing off its sports and casual clothes. Another new feature was 'Sound-Off', where audio consultants carried out professional appraisals of the installation and performance of visitors' audios. One GTI owner, having picked up a set of 15-inch wheels at the Autojumble, was seen fitting them in the car-park and asked if he would sell his 14-inch Pirelli original equipment wheels even before they were off the car.

Above: The only GTI with a 1,000-year rust warranty — a gift from Volkswagen AG to the people of Reifnitz on the shores of the Wörthersee, Austria. The 25-ton Swedish granite block was transported the final 250 metres to this spot by around 1,000 participants in the Sixth International Golf GTI Treffen.

Above: There is no event like the annual Treffen for spotting the latest GTI creations.

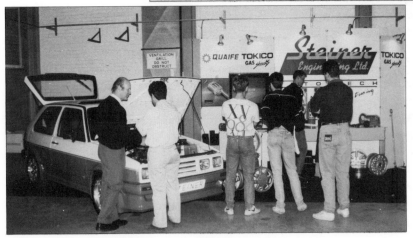

Left : GTI International 1989, and an opportunity to discuss the latest modifications.

12 The Club Scene: Meetings of Like Minds

The area around the town of Glastonbury is known for its esoteric connotations, for its ancient mysteries. Perhaps, then, it is not surprising that it has become the hub of a further esoteric cult — that of the Golf GTI. In the nearby town of Street, allegedly in the giant Zodiac which surrounds the famous tor, lives David Pipes, one of the UK's foremost GTI enthusiasts.

Pipes had previously been a 'Beetle man', his 1.8-litre version benefiting from Wolfrace wheels and the like. From this he transferred to his first Golf GTI, a personal import, black Mk1 1600cc. It was, he recalls, 'luxurious'. By which he means that, unlike the Beetle, it boasted such elements as a decent heater and heated rear window!

He was sufficiently taken by his new purchase to wonder why there was no club for owners of 'such superb cars'. Coincidentally, a letter appeared in *Motor Sport* magazine about that time from Nottingham-based Michael Kingdon, suggesting just such a move. Kingdon — who ran a car valeting business — formed the GTI Drivers Club, with Pipes as one of the original members.

In 1987 Pipes, and around 20 other enthusiasts, decided to visit their first Treffen. Kingdon, who ran the club as a one-man business, was not interested, so Pipes and company decided to 'do their own thing' — complete with Union Jack.

Totally overwhelmed by the event, they returned to the UK and, early in August, held a meeting in Gloucestershire at which they resolved to form their own club. By the end of the afternoon, the name Club GTI had been decided upon, a committee elected — for this was to be a democratic club — and a calendar put together. Stuart Wood, by profession an advertising man, came up with the name and the now well-known badge.

Pipes, newly elected secretary and a member of several Volkswagen clubs during the years he had been driving VWs, was delighted to find that 'GTI drivers really are the friendly, happy bunch of people that I've always found air-cooled drivers to be'.

Half the committee, which now numbers 10, stands down every two years. Pipes became chairman in late 1989. The infectious enthusiasm of those who run the club — in other words, its members — allied to the virtual demise of the GTI Drivers Club which had over 600 members during the mid-1980s, has left Club GTI the pre-eminent association for British Golf GTI owners.

The month following the club's formation, the message was spread from a small stand at VW Action (the annual Volkswagen Owners Club GB event), with another 30 or 40 members joining. Leaflets were left under GTI windscreen wipers, advertisements were placed in the VW specialist magazines, *VW Motoring* and *Volkswagen Audi Car*, and within a year the membership total had risen to over 200.

Today the numbers are into four figures, the total having soared at the turn of the decade. Around 130

Above: These two Golf GTIs are to be found at the home of David Pipes, Club GTI Chairman. On the right is his wife's standard 1990 16V model. On the left is his own, much modified 1989 version.

Left: You can't start too young... David Pipes recruits a Club GTI member for the next century.

Right: Rabbit droppings ruin your paintwork! Vicky Ellison, Club GTI treasurer, and Graham Whittaker, editor, usually keep their furry friend restrained in the back with a set of Volkswagen Motorsport seat-belts.

Left: The modifications on Whittaker and Ellison's Mk2, quaintly known as 'Helga', extend to asymetric Yokohama tyres on BBS RS three-piece modular wheels.

Right: Inside, the Whittaker/Ellison car complements the high standard of the exterior.

Line-up at a GTI sprint — sorry, track day. Note Pete Bull's indecently quick Caddy 16V lurking behind the trio of X-registered Mk1s.

joined at just one GTI International in the early 1990s. 200 membership packs had been prepared for the show — all of them went.

The club's own involvement at that event has included running both the sprint and the slalom. Sprinting is nothing new to the club, which regularly organises its own 'track sessions' at Curborough, near Lichfield, one of the UK's premier sprint courses.

These events have a splendid informality. Not for them the precision of RAC timekeeping, or even the wearing of helmets. Timing is done by good old-fashioned stop-watch and, if the timer's hand slips, well, the member has to have a second run.

There is no pressure on competitors. In fact, 'competitors' is probably the wrong word: 'participants' would be more appropriate. Some would obviously benefit from a day out on the GTI driving course! Up front, however, there is a goodly amount of skill, even if it does perhaps take Tim Stiles and his amazing Mk1 to beat an indecently

quick Volkswagen Caddy to Fastest Time of the Day! Even the odd racing driver, such as Karl Hopkins, can be found enjoying himself 'competing' as a guest of the club. These are that sort of meeting.

By late 1991 David Pipes was on his fifth Golf GTI, and that does not count the two company car GTIs which had been run by his wife, Jan. None has given any trouble. The fifth was a 16V Mk2 which had started life as an Avis fleet car. It now boasts a Stage 1 head from Mark Yates at Mytech Engineering, Koni adjustable shock absorbers, Eibach anti-roll bar, Jetex exhaust, D&W front grille, Pirelli P700Z-shod RH alloys and — a more unusual one, this — a single front wiper arm, courtesy of Bonrath in Germany.

Pipes was the first editor of the club's quarterly magazine, known affectionately as *Rabbit* after the early American Golf. It even includes a 'Rabbit Droppings' section! Knocking this out on his Amstrad word processor obviously gave Pipes the taste for journalism, for he has now given up his job as a buyer in consumer electronics to concentrate on freelance writing, primarily, of course, about the GTI.

The editor's job has since been taken on by Graham Whittaker, a Nottingham design and information technology teacher who was previously responsible for organising club events, including the jaunts to the Treffen

Whittaker and partner Vicky Ellison have also been known to own at least two GTIs at a time — though they have been heard to threaten that one is to be replaced by a highly modified Polo G40! Their jade-green Mk2, registration VAE 167, shows the lengths to which they will go.

The engine is a BRM 180 with a 2-litre Passat 16V block and Schrick camshafts. An Oettinger exhaust system is used, as are an Oettinger headlight grille with Hella DE headlights and Hofele bumper with DE foglights. The exterior is personalised with a Zender Z6 bodykit and Treser rear lighting panel, the interior courtesy of Recaro. Use is made of a Sachs 16V full sports suspension kit, BBS RS 7x15 3-piece wheels, and spectacular, asymmetric Yokohama AVS Dry/Intermediate 195/50ZRx15 tyres. Should one ever get bored driving what Whittaker describes as essentially an *autobahn* cruiser, relief is at hand through the Kenwood stereo system!

The members of Club GTI are split into regional groups. These are very much left to their own devices and can vary according to the character of the members. Functions can range from an evening's ice karting — run by former Golf GTI works rally driver, Simon Davison — to a visit to the Motorway Control Centre near the Severn Bridge. Economy runs, visits to specialist tuners and instruction at the Silverstone Skid School have all been on the menu.

A wide range of merchandise is offered through the club. Discounts are available from all the major GTI tuning companies, while insurance benefits are also included.

The president during the formative years of Club GTI has been Nigel Walker. Until he moved over to Audi in the summer of 1991, Walker had a major say in the image of the GTI in Britain through his post as Volkswagen UK motorsports and marketing manager.

Contact is, course, maintained with clubs overseas, particularly the GTI Club Holland and the Golf GTI Club in Denmark. The former is also a member of the Cologne-based federation of GTI clubs on the Continent, the DGCE (*Dachverband GTI Club Europa*). In Germany, there seems to be a GTI club in virtually every town, some with as few as 25 members.

The majority of DGCE-affiliated clubs are based in Germany, although it also has a number of member clubs in Austria and one each in Switzerland, Holland and Luxembourg. The latter quartet includes the VW Golf GTI Club Oberwallis, the Golf GTI Club Marling and the Golf GTI Club Luxembourg. Total membership of the DGCE is just over 2,000.

National activity tends to centre around the major Volkswagen meetings, the Treffen, of course, being the highlight of the DGCE calendar.

Elsewhere in the world, South Africa, as one might expect, has its own GTi Club of SA, said to be the most motor sport-orientated of all the associations, while American interest tends to be merged into the more conventional Volkswagen clubs — of which there are many in Britain, too. Canada, though, has its Club Golf GTI, and Australia such as the Sydney Golf Club and Golf GTI Club Victoria… Meetings, one might say, of like minds.

Of course they do!

Golf GTI Specifications

Golf GTI Mk1 1.6-litre

Golf GTI Mk1 1.8-litre

Golf GTI Mk2 8-valve

Golf GTI Mk2 16-valve

Golf GTI Mk3

Golf VR6

Golf GTI-powered Reynard Formula 3 Car (1986)

Golf GTI 16V Group A Rally Car (1987)

Golf GTI Mk1 1.6-litre

ENGINE	Four cylinder in line, transversely mounted in front; Bosch K-Jetronic fuel injection
Capacity:	1588cc
Bore/stroke:	79.5mm x 80mm
Output:	110bhp at 6100rpm
Compression ratio:	9.5:1
Maximum torque:	102.9 lbs ft at 5000rpm
TRANSMISSION	Five speed sports gearbox
BRAKES	Internally ventilated discs with servo
TYRES/WHEELS	175/70HR13 on 5½J x 13
DIMENSIONS	
Track front/rear:	1405/1372mm
Wheelbase:	2400mm
Length:	3815mm
Width:	628mm
Height:	1394mm
Unladen weight:	1852lbs
PERFORMANCE	
Top speed:	112mph
Acceleration:	0-60mph 9.1sec
Fuel consumption:	Urban cycle 26.9mpg; constant 56mph 38.2mpg; constant 75mph 29.7mpg

Golf GTI Mk1 1.8-litre

ENGINE	Four cylinder in line, transversely mounted in front; Bosch K-Jetronic fuel injection
Capacity:	1781cc
Bore/stroke:	81mm x 86.4mm
Output:	112bhp at 5800rpm
Compression ratio:	10.0:1
Maximum torque:	109 lbs ft at 3500rpm
TRANSMISSION	Five speed sports gearbox
BRAKES	Diagonally split dual circuit, ventilated discs in front, drum rear, all with servo
TYRES/WHEELS	175/70HR13 on 5½J x 13 alloy
DIMENSIONS	
Track front/rear:	1405mm/1372mm
Wheelbase:	2400mm
Length:	3815mm
Width:	1628mm
Height:	394mm
Unladen weight:	896lbs
PERFORMANCE	
Top speed:	114mph
Acceleration:	0-60mph 8.2sec
Fuel consumption:	Urban cycle 26.6mpg; constant 56mph 47.9mpg; constant 75mph 36.7mpg

Golf GTI Mk2 8-valve

ENGINE	Four cylinder in line, transversely mounted in front; Bosch K-Jetronic fuel injection
Capacity:	1781cc
Bore/stroke:	81mm x 86.4mm
Output:	112bhp at 5500rpm
Compression ratio:	10.0:1
Maximum torque:	114 lbs ft at 3100rpm
TRANSMISSION	Five speed sports gearbox
BRAKES	Diagonally split dual circuit, discs front and rear, ventilated discs in front, all with servo
TYRES/WHEELS	185/60HR14 on 6J x 14
DIMENSIONS	
Track front/rear:	1422/1422mm
Wheelbase:	2464mm
Length:	3988mm
Width:	1676mm
Height:	1397mm
Unladen weight:	3-door 2028lbs; 5-door 2072lbs
PERFORMANCE	
Top speed:	119mph
Acceleration:	0-60mph 8.3sec
Fuel consumption:	Urban cycle 27.4mpg; constant 56mph 48.7mpg; constant 75mph 37.2mpg

Golf GTI Mk2 16-valve

ENGINE	Four cylinder in line, transversely mounted in front; Bosch K-Jetronic fuel injection
Capacity:	1781cc
Bore/stroke:	81mm x 86.4mm
Output:	139bhp at 6100rpm
Compression ratio:	10.0:1
Maximum torque:	168Nm at 4600rpm
TRANSMISSION	Five speed sports gearbox
BRAKES	Diagonally split dual circuit, discs front and rear, all with servo
TYRES/WHEELS	185/60VR14 on 6J x 14 steel
DIMENSIONS	
Track front/rear:	1422/1422mm
Wheelbase:	2464mm
Length:	3988mm
Width:	1676mm
Height:	1397mm
Unladen weight:	2116lbs
PERFORMANCE	
Top speed:	129mph
Acceleration:	0-62mph 8.5sec
Fuel consumption:	Urban cycle 25.9mpg; constant 56mph 46.4mpg; constant 75mph 37.8mpg

Golf GTI Mk 3

ENGINE	Four cylinder in line, transversely mounted in front; Bosch Digifant ignition and injection system
Capacity:	1984cc
Bore/stroke:	82.5 x 92.8mm
Output:	115bhp at 5400rpm
Compression ratio:	10.4:1
Maximum torque:	166Nm at 3200rpm
BRAKES	Diagonally split dual circuit, internally ventilated discs with servo
TYRES/WHEELS	195/50R15V on 6Jx15
DIMENSIONS	
Track front/rear:	1462/1444mm
Wheelbase:	2475mm
Length:	4020mm
Width:	1710mm
Height:	1405mm
Unladen weight:	3-door 2282lbs; 5-door 2337lbs
PERFORMANCE	
Top speed:	123mph
Acceleration:	0-62mph 10.1sec
Fuel consumption:	Urban cycle 27.37mpg; constant 56mph 48.56mpg; constant 75mph 38.60mpg

Golf VR6

ENGINE	Six cylinder VR, transversely mounted in front; Bosch Motronic ignition and injection system
Capacity:	2792cc
Bore/stroke:	81 x 90.3mm
Output:	174bhp at 5800rpm
Compression ratio:	10.0:1
Maximum torque:	235Nm at 4200rpm
BRAKES	Diagonally split dual circuit, internally ventilated discs with ABS/EDS
TYRES/WHEELS	205/50R15V on 6½J x 15
DIMENSIONS	
Track front/rear:	1450/1434mm
Wheelbase:	2475mm
Length:	4020mm
Width:	1710mm
Height:	1405mm
Unladen weight:	3-door 2546lbs; 5-door 2601lbs
PERFORMANCE	
Top speed:	140mph
Acceleration:	0-62mph 7.6sec
Fuel consumption:	Urban cycle 22.93mpg; constant 56mph 38.60mpg; constant 75mpg 32.21mpg

1986 Golf GTI-powered Reynard Formula Three Car

ENGINE	Four cylinder in line, longitudinally installed in front of rear axle. Light alloy crossflow cylinder head. Squish combustion.
Capacity:	1999cc
Bore/stroke:	82.25 x 94mm
Output:	162bhp at 5400rpm
Compression ratio:	11.5:1
Maximum torque:	164 lbs ft at 5000rpm
Valve gear:	Overhead camshaft, bucket tappets
Fuel system:	Lucas mechanical fuel injection
Ignition:	Luminition electronic
Fuel grade:	Premium
TRANSMISSION	AP twin plate racing clutch; Hewland five speed close ratio gearbox
BRAKES	11in solid discs front and rear
BATTERY	Varley
RUNNING GEAR	Front axle: twin wishbones, anti-roll bar, pushrods with inboard coiled dampers; rear axle: twin wishbones, pushrods with inboard coiled dampers; steering: rack and pinion
TYRES	Front 180/500 13; rear 225/550 13
WHEELS	Alloy 8in front 10in rear

1987 Golf GTI 16V Group A Rally Car

ENGINE	Four cylinder, 4 valves per cylinder, fitted with high compression pistons
Capacity:	1781cc
Bore/stroke:	81 x 86.4mm
Output:	200bhp at 7500rpm
Compression ratio:	10.0:1
Fuel system:	Bosch K-Jetronic
Ignition:	Transistorised
Lubrication:	Wet sump
Clutch:	Single plate
TRANSMISSION	Strengthened close ratio five speed gearbox with limited slip differential
SUSPENSION	Sachs gas pressured height adjustable shock absorbers
WHEELS	Ronal alloy, 6J x 15 on gravel, 7J x 15 on tarmac
BRAKES	Ventilated AP racing discs front, standard discs rear
PETROL TANK	17.6 gallon safety fuel cell
SAFETY EQUIPMENT	Matter roll cage; Recaro competition seats; alloy sump guards; Sabelt seat belts; fire extinguisher system
WEIGHT	1940lbs
SUPPLIERS	Tyres — Michelin; oil — Shell; plugs — various; shock absorbers — Sachs; clutch — Sachs; lamps — Hella; brake material — various

The author

Born on the production line at Cowley and brought up in the back of a Morris 8, Ian Wagstaff has been writing for motoring magazines throughout his working life. He started by contributing race reports to *Motoring News*, *Autosport* and others, eventually spending a year as press and promotions manager for Silverstone Circuits. Realising that motor racing meant getting up early on Sunday mornings, he transferred his attention to automotive parts and accessories, becoming editor of the business journal, *Auto Accessory Retailer*. He went out on his own in 1984, becoming one of the country's leading automotive trade press freelances.

Besides contributing to trade magazines in the UK, Europe and the USA, he also writes for a number of consumer magazines including *Auto Express*, *Practical Motorist* and *VW Motoring*, for whom he spent some years as News and Motor Sport Editor. It was in this last capacity that he was able to keep a close eye on the recent development of the Golf GTI.

Ian is also an automotive consultant to The Economist Intelligence Unit, for whom he has written Special Reports on the UK Replacement Parts Market. It was in connection with the first of these that, in 1986, Renault presented him with its Pierre Dreyfus Award, given to the member of The Guild of Motoring Writers 'judged to have made the most outstanding journalistic effort during the year'.

His second book — *Classics in Colour: Volkswagen Golf GTI* —is currently in preparation.